The Day of the Saxon

Homer Lea

Simon Publications
2003

First published in 1912 by Harper & Brothers, New York, London

Library of Congress Card Number: 12014979

ISBN: 1-932512-02-0

Published by Simon Publications, Inc. P. O. Box 910455, San Diego, CA 92191-0455

TO
FIELD-MARSHAL LORD ROBERTS
V. C., K. G.

CONTENTS

CHAP.   PAGE

PREFACE ix

BOOK I

I. THE SAXON AND HIS EMPIRE 1

II. THE BRITISH EMPIRE AND WAR 6

III. THE SAXON AND AMERICA 25

IV. THE SAXON AND INDIA 44

V. THE SAXON AND INDIA (CONTINUED) 54

VI. THE SAXON AND THE PACIFIC 66

VII. THE SAXON AND EASTERN ASIA 82

VIII. THE SAXON AND THE RUSSIAN 100

IX. THE SAXON AND EUROPE 119

X. THE SAXON AND THE GERMANS 129

BOOK II

I. THE BRITISH EMPIRE AND THE WORLD 149

II. LIMITATIONS OF NAVAL WARFARE 164

III. LIMITATIONS OF NAVAL WARFARE (CONTINUED) . . 173

IV. SAXON STRUGGLE FOR SURVIVAL—RUSSIA 186

V. SAXON STRUGGLE FOR SURVIVAL—GERMANY 202

VI. PREPARATION AND CONFLICT 216

VII. UNITY OF FORCES 230

INDEX 243

LIST OF CHARTS

Chart I . . . . *Facing p.* 64
Chart II . . . . " 78
Chart III . . . . " 112
Chart IV . . . . " 142

PREFACE

THIS is the second volume of that work dealing with new phases of military science as they affect national existence which has occupied my time for several years past. The first volume was *The Valor of Ignorance;* the third is not yet completed.

I have many persons to thank for the interest they have shown in the progress of this volume, and I wish particularly to thank Sir John George Tollemache Sinclair, Bart. of Thurso Castle, who has been most kind in securing various data, etc., for me.

This book has been written under numerous difficulties. Begun in America, parts were written upon every continent and every sea, being finally completed in Asia. Begun in profound peace, the concluding chapters were finished upon a recent field of battle.

H. L.

NANKING, CHINA.

BOOK I

It is a law of nature common to all mankind, which no time shall annul or destroy, that those who have more strength and excellence shall bear rule over those who have less.—DIONYSIUS.

THE DAY OF THE SAXON

I

THE SAXON AND HIS EMPIRE

Origin of National Disintegration.—Degree of War.—Old and New
Patriotism.

WHEN we consider interests vital to national existence we can differentiate but slightly between them and the personal wants that control individual efforts. Both are moved by the same impulses, and over both the same wide vanities and fears hold dominion. Nations are not introspective any more than are individuals, and the degree that crises affect them is determined inversely by the remoteness in time and space of their occurrence. What has happened in the past or what may take place in the future, what goes on without the threshold or beyond the boundaries of the state, has little effect upon mankind as compared with the influence of internal affairs and the domestic concerns of the present.

THE DAY OF THE SAXON

In the circumscription of man's fealty to his immediate time and environment is to be found the origin of all national and racial disintegration. When men abandon with reluctance their own dunghills for the glories of their God, the fretful moments of their existence for the calm of eternal time, how fragile are their racial bonds and how futile are the hopes based upon them!

By the efforts men make to preserve their families from want, from servitude or destruction do we judge their domestic virtues. In such a manner, only to a larger degree, should judgment be rendered upon these same men according to the efforts they make toward a like preservation of their race. If a man who gives over his family to the vicissitudes of his neglect is deserving of scorn, how great should be the contempt felt for him who evades the obligations he owes his race and gives over, not alone his family, but all his people to conquest or destruction.

Public fealty is only a nobler conception of the duty a man owes his family. A nation is a union of families; patriotism the synthesis of their domestic virtues. The ruin of states, like the ruin of families, comes from one cause—neglect. To neglect one's family is to lose it; to neglect one's country is to perish with it. Individuals are a part of the world only in the duration or memory of their race.

The British Empire stands in the same relation to this neglect, its causes and results, as all other nations that have gone down because of it. Wars have brought about the formation of this Empire; and wars will prolong or shorten its existence according as to whether or not the British people prepare for those inevitable struggles that are now approaching and which belong in no way to the ephemeral ordinances or the passions of men but are a part of those elemental forces that take no cognizance of mankind nor of his institutions.

Factors that determine the length or brevity of wars are invariable in their application, and the conditions circumscribing the military relationship of the Empire to the world are reducible to three principles:

1. When the military preparedness of the British Empire is developed proportionately to that of its strongest enemy and continues in constant progression during peace, the number of its wars, their duration and destruction of life, is reduced to a minimum.

2. Whenever its state of military preparedness is only equal to the least militant power, then it is capable of waging war only with such a nation. These wars are the longest in duration and are the greatest in the destruction of life and property.

3. When a state of military preparedness is highly developed in the enemy and lacking in the British Empire, the destruction of the Empire will ensue if that attack is developed in Europe against the United Kingdom or is directed against the Indian frontiers.

The British Empire will be destroyed only through those avertable causes which the Saxon now dreads to contemplate. Yet it is because of this evasion that the defense of the Empire falls away and the time of its dissolution draws near.

To understand the true significance of an empire as vast and fragile as that of the Saxon one must have no fixed opinions concerning its military progression, but must, on the other hand, make the acquisition of such knowledge the basic principle of his patriotism.

The Saxon has marked around this earth, as has no other race before him, the scarlet circle of his power. This thin, red Saxon line, so thin with his numbers, so red with his blood, was made possible only by his heroism and racial fealty. Where this line has not gone man has not found. It has crossed every sea; it has traversed every desert; it has sought every solitude; it has passed through swamps where only the sacred ibis fishes; over sands that have never been moistened; over snows that have never melted. There has been no storm it has not encountered, no pain it has not endured; no race it has not fought, and no disease it has not contended with. This Saxon line has been to the earth a girdle tragic and heroic, binding within itself all the old and great places of the world. It has been silent in its duty, ignored in its achievement, and scorned in its devotion; yet it has given down to this now neglectful race a world such as mankind has never known before; an empire over which the sun and stars shine together; where night never falls nor dawn begins.

At this late hour or never must the Saxon people arouse themselves to the somber consequences of their neglect and break away from the pleasant security of their delusions. To them has now come that gloomy dawn so familiar to man throughout all the nights and dawns he has bedded and risen together, falling asleep upon a peaceful earth and getting up to find it a place of strife; going to bed under the serene and happy heavens and awakening to find them filled with demons; laying his head upon the pillow of his gods and rising to find himself abandoned. This has ever been the fate of nations as they have laid themselves down to sleep throughout the ages much in the same manner as the Saxon race, in all their glory and hope and vanity, only to awake at a predetermined hour to find themselves upon a savage dawn, stripped and desolate.

II

THE BRITISH EMPIRE AND WAR

War Basic Principle in National Progression.—Preparation Constant in Change.—Determination of Source and Approximate Time of Simple.—Law of Survival Immutable.—British Empire Made from Fragments of Four Powers.—Now Confronted by Four.—Laws Governing Future Decisive Hostilities.—Militancy Divisible into Three Phases.—Duration of Peace.—Application to British Empire.

THE scorn of war, like the denial of death, belongs to the same category of self-deception. It is the derision of the non-apparent. It is the hate of hateful realities. So mankind hides it away from himself in those deeper cellars of his consciousness where, all heaped together, are secreted his hidden fears. National valor based on concealment is no more than the spontaneous expression of national fears, the mad struggle of them under the propulsion of necessity. To evade the contemplation of individual extinction is identical, in a general sense, with that subterfuge practised by unmartial nations toward war. The inevitability of both is recognized, but the application of this knowledge is relegated, not to themselves, but to all other men and all other nations.

THE BRITISH EMPIRE AND WAR

War is a part of life, and its place in national existence is fixed and predetermined. Human equivocation cannot affect its status; nor the laws of mankind its application. To the degree that war is a basic principle in national progression must preparation for its conduct be specific. There can be no scorn of it, nor denial, nor fear, nor the substitution of human ordinances for those that are cognizant of man only in the aggregate.

While the policy of statesmen in one generation may affect, for good or for evil, the affairs of the nation in a distant period of time, there still exists, nevertheless, that effective counterpoise of constant readjustment of international relationship that is determined, not by the statesmen themselves, but by external conditions over which they have no control and from which they have no defense except to readjust their policies and systems.

In this manner, and no other, must the conduct of a nation's military policy be carried on. The same external control remains paramount and constant; and, as the probabilities of war shift from one nation to another, preparations must shift accordingly; a state of preparedness must always exist that is variable yet specific.

This fundamental principle is denied by the British Empire in its military development, as it is by America and China. The latter is now paying the price of its scorn; and, though the penalty has not as yet been exacted from America and the

British Empire, the time is near at hand when the old Shylock of their disdain shall bare the breasts of both.

To the multitude of a nation engrossed in their own affairs it seems impossible to foretell the approach of war, the place from which it shall come and the manner of its conflict. Hence it is that in nations governed by popular will the preparation for war is, according to the degree that the populace controls such legislation, general in character and useless in application.

In the formative processes of national life and in their eventual dissolution there is nothing uncertain nor mysterious in the determination of the quarter from whence wars shall come nor the approximate time of their approach. But whenever legislation affecting war is determined by popular will, such legislation becomes incoherent; when controlled by constitutional limitations, it becomes inflexible and passes into a state of dry rot. Like the puff-ball, it retains its outward semblance, yet the heart of it is no more than dust.

When we consider that characteristic now so predominant in the nations of the Anglo-Saxon race, of allowing individual wants to take precedence over the vital interests of national existence, we find in it every source of militant immobility and decay.

The sun never sets on the same political and military conditions that its first rays illumine. The rapidity of this diurnal change is not apparent to man, sunk in his own affairs, for he views the progression of national and worldly events—if he views them at all—in the same manner as he regards, unconcernedly and concretely, the drift of the stream. He is cognizant of it only as a whole. Yet it is the unnumbered minute particles that constitute its volume and their ceaseless surging that determines its movement. As a river viewed from a distance appears an immovable mass, so in like manner does the individual of Anglo-Saxon nations regard the flow and volume of national events. It is because of this that their military systems have become fixed; whereas, if state and race are to survive, their flexibility should be in constant ratio to the causes that determine their institution.

The British Empire stands in no different relation to these elemental characteristics of warfare than any other nation that has ever existed, though the utilization of its military power, governed by different conditions, may bear but little resemblance to the military activities of other nations. We are not at present concerned with the expression of British militancy, but only with its constitution and the fundamental principles that govern its relationship to the continuance and preservation of the Empire.

Bitter as the realization of it may be, bitter as is the contemplation of national fragility and the futile struggle of man to find refuge in the delusion of universal peace, the natural law of survival remains immutable. The Saxon Empire can endure only so long as her military development remains constant to her political expansion and the economic development of her territories. This military development moreover must be proportionate to the military, political, and commercial expansion of all other nations, singly and in coalition. Never, so long as their expansion, whether militant, political, or economic, is convergent with the Empire's established interests, can British militancy remain dormant or evade its responsibilities.

The same causes and the identical means that brought about the establishment of all other nations produced in like manner the British Empire. By wars and conquests, by theft and intrigue, by the same brutal use of physical power, was it put together piece by piece.

The brutality of all national development is apparent, and we make no excuse for it. To conceal it would be a denial of fact; to glamour it over, an apology to truth. There is little in life that is not brutal except our ideal. As we increase the aggregate of individuals and their collective activities, we increase proportionately their brutality.

Nations cannot be created, nor can they become great, by any purely ethical or spiritual expansion. The establishment, in great or small entities, of tribes and states is the resultant only of their physical power; and whenever there is a reversal, or an attempted reversal to this, the result is either internal dissolution or sudden destruction, their dismembered territories going to make up the dominions of their conquerors.

In just such a manner has the British Empire been made up from the fragments of four great maritime powers; the satrapies of petty potentates and the wilderness of nameless savages.

When the commercial power of Venice and Genoa passed over to Portugal and Spain, these two powers had, by their discoveries and conquest, divided, in a practical sense, the world between them. Yet the militant decay began early to manifest itself in Portugal, and by the end of the melancholy reign of John III. it had made its final exit from the camps of dominant kingdoms. In like manner Spain began to go down after the revolt of the Netherlands.

Holland, France, and England then assumed the power of these two decadent states in the same manner as they had taken over the abandoned possessions of other states and tribes.

It was not until after the Peace of Bredo that the decline of Holland began, discordant, desperate, inevitable. It suffered from the old disease of nations, that universal paresis, the delusion that trade and its gold constitutes a national asset capable of indefinite progression, and is freed from concomitant military expansion. So it descended from the dais of its greatness and now sits in the shadow of other kingdoms' footstools — a jester in the motley of universal peace.

The going down of Holland was followed by that of France, beginning subsequent to the Seven Years' War and ending in the days of the Revolution. With the decline of France as a maritime power, continental supremacy upon the sea was at an end. By the close of the eighteenth century England had gathered together the wreckage of these nations—the wreckage for which she was not alone responsible. By their vanity and ignorance, by her valor and brutality—as is the way of nations—she seized, one by one, their seas and dominions.

Now, after a century of rule, of such supremacy as mankind has never heretofore known, the British Empire is confronted, not by one, but by four powers in the eventual struggle for the suzerainty of one-third the world. Each of these nations is proportionately better qualified to wrest it from the Saxons than were they, from the middle of the sixteenth to the end of the eighteenth century, capable of taking it by force of arms from Portugal, Spain, Holland, and France.

It is not, however, in the military potentiality of these Powers that the dread of the Briton should be found, but rather in the fundamental difference that exists between the conquests of the sixteenth and the twentieth centuries. In those earlier centuries the hunt and bagging of states was rather the result of individual lust for individual loot and was, in consequence, restricted. Now all is changed; the individual has given way to his composite self, the nation, and the loot of town and tavern has given way to the universal thievery of natural resources that modern civilization has made necessary for the progression of man and the supremacy of his political institutions. In those old days it was the orderless strife of individuals; now it is the predetermined struggle of nations. In those times when the world was opulent and the greed of man was the small greed of his single self, mankind marauded rather than warred. Now it is the struggle of nations in the last looting of Nature; increasing each year in intensity, not alone by the added increment of population, but by the development of material science and the growing hungers of our insatiable civilization.

The two laws that govern in the future the outbreak of decisive hostilities, we state as follows:

1. When the resources of one nation stand in inverse ratio to its military power, and the military capacity of its competitor is proportionate to the needs of its race, then war will ensue when the military decadence of one and the economic necessities of the other reach a known point.

2. When the exploitation of the natural resources of a nation militarily weak is prohibitive to nations militarily strong, war will ensue when the economic needs of the militant powers exceed their own natural resources.

It is in these two principles that is found the true source and terribleness of those wars that must in due time fall upon the British Empire.

The inevitability of wars cannot be determined upon by the extraneous manifestations of their precipitating causes. These causes have nothing to do with the source of war and, strange as it may seem, have only the slightest effect upon the combat itself. The sources of war are constant and immutable, differing only in the viewpoint of the observer, while the apparent and precipitating causes are no more than ephemeral, coming and going from time to time, as the fluttering of smoke over some crater-top. Yet it is upon this coming and going of the immaterial that the false doctrine of arbitration is based.

As the complexity of civilization increases, with a corresponding augmentation of popular control in governmental affairs, the personal element in warfare vanishes. In future wars the rages of kings and the schemes of their ministers will play no part; their origin now rests in the contact of nations and races, in the convergence of their expansion. Due to this fact, that uncertain element, the hates of monarchs and the ambitions of their ministers, is eliminated, and the determination of the approach of war becomes more exact. We have already enunciated the law governing the convergence of nations.[1]

The basic principle of war has been the same for all time and will continue so until the end of human contention. Only the immediate causes and manner

[1] *The Valor of Ignorance.*

of war, those last straws that break down the peace of nations, alter from age to age. In the past it was the individual who was the predominant factor; to-day, nations; to-morrow, races.

It is in the political and geographical situation of the British Empire that we must look to its freedom from war or its position as the storm-center of those terrible struggles that must fall upon the world sometime on the morrow.

In exact proportion as the Empire is removed from the expanding spheres of other nations will it be freed from the environment of combat; but to the degree that the reverse is true the Empire is placed within the sphere of war.

The character of the British Dominion is different from any of the great empires that have preceded it. It not only consists of one-fourth the land surface, but the suzerainty of the Five Seas. It is over this seventeen-twentieths of the world that broods the jealous yet anxious scowl of the Saxon race. That British rule should, in various degrees of sovereignty, exercise its dominion over seventeen-twentieths of the world's surface is significant of just that degree of repression toward all other nations, their rights and expansion by land or by sea.

It is not so much in the vastness of British possessions that are found conditions provocative of war as it is in its geographical distribution. It is not a segregated sovereignty occupying, as the Russian Empire, a corner or contiguous portion of the earth, but forms, on the other hand, a circle around the entire globe, within which is placed all the other powers of the world; and not one of them can follow their lines of natural expansion without, sooner or later, being brought into direct contact with the British Dominion.

It is not for us to comment on this portentous circle, this stupendous yet shadowy girdle, that holds for the human race so much of terror and of gratitude, so much of freedom and of war. It is enough to make evident its presence and its potentialities.

At the present time no great nation in Europe or Asia can move on those radii of expansion, as determined by natural law, radii upon which they must move or fall into decadence, without the prior destruction of Saxon sovereignty. It is because of this that we find in Europe more than sixteen million soldiers and in Asia more than three millions to break forth at some predetermined time, singly or in coalition, and shatter the vast yet fragile circle of British power.

As we contemplate the Saxon armies of less than half a million men, scattered around the world on this never-ending circle under the pretense of guarding against twice ten million men, there is recalled to us a similar scene that one may look upon from the northern slopes of the Wu Tai Mountains, where the old wall of China stretches like the British wall over dominions it can no longer defend. Over mountain chains, through deserts, across rivers, around principalities and states it goes on and on until one would almost imagine that there was neither end nor beginning to it. But alas, the end of the wall is there; there at every point upon which the eye rests. It is no longer a wall: it is a monument.

So now as we meditate upon the living wall of Britain, extending not across a northern frontier, but around and around the world, we see only the present in its counterpart of antiquity. Like the old wall of Hoangti, its watch towers have crumbled, but man rather than time has thrown them down. The Saxon himself, and not the enemy, has put out its watch-fires, torn down its merlons, and made the wide breaches between its bastions. It is no longer a barrier, but, not unlike the old wall of China, it is a monument, a monument to the dead that built it and to the spirit that has all but departed.

We have, heretofore, found that the militancy of a race is primarily dependent upon necessity; and, as this condition passes, the militancy dependent upon it deteriorates; and, while the necessity of militancy must return to a race at some subsequent period, the militant spirit does not return simultaneously with it. Because of this single tragic fact, do nations, whenever they reach such pre-eminence among other states as to appear to themselves impregnable, sanction the degeneration of the military spirit. When this decadence reaches a certain point, the nation, regardless of its wealth, area, or population is destroyed.

Militancy is divisible into three distinct phases:

1. The militancy of the struggle to survive.

2. The militancy of conquest.

3. The militancy of supremacy or preservation of ownership.

It is in the first that the military genius of a people reaches its height. It is in the last that the nation takes its final departure from the affairs of mankind.

The Saxon race has apparently entered upon this last stage of militancy. The old ideals that made possible the Empire have been put aside. The militant spirit has become of secondary consideration: it is now hardly more than that spirit of the trade rat, redolent and satisfied in the accumulation of that which is useless to national and racial progression.

It is, therefore, the purpose of this work to examine into, not alone the probabilities of war that must eventually result in the destruction of the Empire, but into the possibilities of bringing about a militant renascence of the Saxon race before their day is finally done.

We have considered in a general sense the main factors that determine the militant decadence of a race or state, but we have omitted one salient factor —the control by statesmen over the direction of national progression, national ideals and institutions. This control, paradoxical as it may seem, diminishes as is increased the power of the populace over governmental affairs. No people are more easily deceived than when permitted to deceive themselves. Self-deception is the rule of the human race. Hence in any government dependent upon the will of the populace statesmen give way to politicians, and these, so notorious for their cowardly nature, go with the populace along the line of least resistance. In national affairs this line leads to the most debased of ideals—the supremacy of individual greed over national unity and perpetuation.

Had British statesmen at the close of the militant era of conquest taken the precaution to preserve Saxon militancy in its purity, and held it aloof from the sweat and hypocrisy of commercial supremacy, there would not now exist those dangers we are to consider in this work.

It is true that even the wisest statesmen, being but transient in their tenure of office, resort to expedients. But the mediocre statesman gives no thought to the true relation the state and its functions bear to the individual. Whenever they differentiate between them in the discharge of their duties, the future gives way to the present and the nation to the individual.

As the power of the populace increases, the wisdom of the statesmen, who concern themselves with external affairs, decreases proportionately. Because of this it is no uncommon thing to find that their judgment relative to war is not superior to the common opinion of their constituents. Instead of being cognizant of the one primitive principle that the expansion of nations and their concomitant wars are governed by natural laws, they construe these laws and wars to be of their own making, since the forces productive of them operate through their agency.

So now in this crucial period of the Saxon race we find it given over to self-deception, to the fat somnolence of satisfaction, viewing all the world that lies beyond their shadow with complaisance and obese disdain. Party politics, obscuring the nation in its yellow mist, endeavors to form within this fleeting nebulosity a world of its own, filling it with all that is temporizing and false, all that is transient and corrodent, until that eventual day when the storm of war shall scatter this nebula of fraud and the world shall find it a worm-eaten pile in the cleared wash of its sea.

Wars against the British Empire are not governed by conditions mysterious nor unknown, but are, on the other hand, determinable with more or less exactitude; and our purpose in this work is to examine into the occurrence of those conflicts that must ensue so long as the Saxon Empire encircles the world.

The determination of future wars directed against the Saxon race is governed by four definite principles.

1. There can be no salient political or territorial expansion of any of the great powers without a corresponding subtraction from British Dominion. The degree of this subtraction or destruction, as the

case may be, is determined by the relative disproportion between the military capacity of the expanding powers and that of the Empire.

2. War by a single power against the Empire, in ascertaining its probability and time, is determined by the rate of the expansion along one or more radii converging upon the British Dominion, plus the momentum of national necessity and the kinetic energy of its military establishment.

3. War by a coalition against the Empire is determined by the approximation of their equality in rates of expansion along their respective radii convergent on specific arcs of the British circle, plus their approximate equality in national momentum and military energy.

4. The number of allies is determined by three factors:

(a) The time of mutual adjustment.

(b) The degree of weakness in two or more arcs of the British circle.

(c) The degree of militant expansion of two or more nations whose respective radii are convergent upon the two or more weakened arcs in the British circle.

Preparation for the continuance of the Empire and the preservation of its integrity must be specific. It must be as ceaseless and expanding as is the progression of the race itself. The Imperial circle with which the Saxon has girdled the world—and mankind—is not fixed, but is, on the other hand, in a

state of constant agitation. This alternating shrinkage and expansion is the Law of Nations. Frontiers
are never, but for the briefest period of time, quies-
cent. Hence it is that, in seeking the approximately
constant variation in national boundaries in order
to ascertain whether their tendency is to contract or
extend, we do not look to their geographical borders,
but to the spirit of their people.

Each nation builds its own monuments—and
writes its own epitaphs.

If, however, we regard only the geographical and
political situation of the Empire we find that it
stands in relation to the powers of the world, not
only productive of the possibility and probability
of war, but the absolute certainty of it. Yet this
is not the end; for, when the spirit of the nation
breaks forth at the same time in the denial of war,
then we have not war, but destruction. This denial
means nothing more nor less than a belief on their
part that the world acquiesces in Saxon sovereignty;
the spontaneous shrinkage of their own countries
and the unopposed expansion of the British Empire
until it assumes the undisputed sovereignty of the
world.

For a Saxon to deny war is to epitomize human
vanity.

Peace and its duration, like war, is determined by
natural laws that in their fundamental principles
do not vary nor are found wanting.

In conformity to these laws we find that the future

peace of the Empire stands in decreasing ratio and must so continue until it is either destroyed or reaches a point of world dominance.

There can be no further extension of British sovereignty without encroachment upon the political rights and territorial possessions of other nations—a condition of warfare the continuity of which is determined by the relative equality in military power that exists between the Empire and the nations that stand across its lines of expansion.

There can be no retention of present British sovereignty without the repression of the territorial and political expansion of other nations—a condition that must culminate in war, one war if the Empire is destroyed; a series if it is victorious.

The intensity of these conditions increases with each year of added population; each year of augmented arts and sciences that open up to mankind new wants, while at the same time diminishing the source of their supply; each year of new invention that shatters time and space and crowds the greater nations, by irresistible and uncontrollable expansion, against the circle of the British Empire.

It is in this last principle that we come upon the inevitability of war, upon the full consciousness of it, so that no amount of hope nor evasion nor denial can conceal it from us. It is very simple, this irrevocable law of war. It is terrible in its simplicity.

The circle of the Saxon Dominion must be broken or the greatness of other nations be restricted.

Their growth, their ideals, and aspirations must, on reaching it, stop; and in that stoppage, decline; in that going down, perish. But this condition can only result after long and terrible struggles, after they have been hurled back from the Saxon circle into their own small corner of the world. Should, however, these nations not be hurled back, then the circle is shattered, and other nations assume supremacy, each in its respective arc, over those dominions of the Saxon race.

In this epoch of war upon which the Empire is about to enter, hopes of peace are futile; constitutions and kings and gods are without avail, for these are the old, old struggles that govern the growth and dissolution of national life.

III

THE SAXON AND AMERICA

Principles Governing Political Relationship of Nations.—Inter-relationship between British Empire and the World.—Principles Governing Break-up of a Scattered Empire.—Future Relation to America.—Sources of Future Canadian Population.—Its Effect.—United States No Longer a Saxon Nation.—Degrees of Expansion.—England has Maintained Doctrine of American Immunity.—Military Superiority Necessary.

CONDITIONS that determine and factors that govern political relationship between nations appear, in the multiplicity of transient stipulation, to be both intricate and subtle. This is a delusion built up by the vanity of man, as in former times he believed himself to be the center of the universe; the earth his barnyard, the sun his bonfire, the moon and stars his big and little candles, all of which had been arranged for him by the same Creator who stalked patiently in his foot-steps to note down his meritorious deeds and to wink at his shortcomings.

The political relationship that exists among nations, far from being complex, is reducible to two general principles. But man, through whom these principles must find expression, instead of acknowledging his true relationship as the agency through whom they must act, endeavors to attribute to himself a creative faculty and would have himself believe that in him and his momentary tenure upon earth rests the origin of all the immutable laws that regulate nations in their wars and in peace.

The added years of human life upon earth and the vast increasing sums of empirical knowledge never bring mankind to realize that he cannot circumvent those irrevocable decrees of human association, either individually or collectively. These belong not to him, but to Nature.

Man should be as old as recorded time, yet he remains, whenever his vanity intervenes, as young as his own years.

The wisdom of the human race only finds expression in the ignorance of the individual.

The cumulative wisdom of the world has, in practical workings, little effect in guiding the destiny of nations even in this age of superior intelligence. It can be truly said that, while we are two thousand years older than Cæsar, we have statesmen whose political intelligence antedates that historical period by an almost equal number of years.

A nation retrogrades in universal political intelligence in proportion as its international affairs are controlled by popular prejudice. The understanding of the populace concerning matters remote from their immediate environment is the comprehension, not of their maximum individual intelligence, but of their maximum collective ignorance. Foreign policies, like the hopes and terrors of the unknown, are without the realm of popular reason. This is due not alone to ignorance, but to the supervention of the present over both the past and the future, to the domination of an immediate environment over the possibilities or dangers of an horizon concerning which little or nothing is known. The limitations of the individual are very great.

The common man loves his own dunghill better than heaven.

All activity, human or otherwise, that is constant in its recurrence, identical in its causes and effects, indifferent to time or geographical segregation, is governed by universal law. But when concerned with mankind and the diverse interests that affect him, the invariability of these principles is overlooked; or rather, as the proverbial grains of wheat, they are hid under shifting clouds of human chaff.

The two principles, one positive and the other negative, that govern concretely the political relationship of nations may be stated:

1. The duration of national existence depends upon a nation's physical power to remain or become supreme over other political entities whose interests are convergent.

2. A nation's physical power must remain constant in its capacity to prevent dictation, conquest, or supremacy by other states whose interests are convergent.

These two laws constitute and exemplify the

fundamental principles that govern the political relationship of nations. All other conditions of national existence and innumerable phases of their application are subordinate. So long as these two principles are conserved and applied in their entirety to national progression, statesmen need not concern themselves with secondary factors, for they will fall naturally into their allotted and circumscribed spheres.

These are the principles that must guide us in the examination of the political relationship the British Empire bears to the rest of the world.

The ascertainment of the political interrelationship existent between the British Empire and the balance of the world is first determinable by the relationship of their lines of expansion and shrinkage; the acuteness of their angles of convergence and the kinetic energy by which they move along these lines. While we cannot, in the brevity of this work, take up each nation and consider the conditions that govern its expansion or shrinkage and affect, in a correlative degree, the British Empire, we will do so, in a broader sense, considering first America, then Asia and Europe, in order that the true political contact of the Saxon race with those nations may be understood in its gloomy and portentous phases.

The early British struggles in the Western Hemisphere show decisively those changeless elements that determine national expansion and retrogression. In that contact and in the strife that accompanied it are portrayed not only the three degrees of militancy already considered, but resultant conditions that are in themselves prognostications of an inevitable end.

The loss of the American Colonies, due, not so much to the American Revolution, as to the ignorance of British statesmen and the concurrence of European wars, is illustrative of two quite opposite principles in the break-up of an empire whose territories are not contiguous. The same principles hold true at the present time, and the dangers inherent in them are always existent.

1. The convergence of one or more nations upon a single frontier may cause the loss of dominions in quite the opposite part of the empire. This results when the military equilibrium of all frontiers is not properly maintained.

2. The segregated portions of an empire whose dominions are separated by seas, acquire, in proportion to the time they have become an established community, interests that are distinct from those of the empire as a whole. When these conditions become as decisive as those that resulted in the separation of the American Colonies, then that portion of the empire affected invariably makes common cause with those nations whose convergence of interests has reached, concurrently, an identical acuteness.

While we will not make conclusive application of these principles until toward the close of this work,

we have, nevertheless, given this early expression to
.them that they may always be kept in mind, for
they form two links in the great chain that must
bind the empire together.

The political relationship of the British Empire
toward America in the future, increasing in decisiveness with each decade, must be considered from three
salient points:

1. Convergence of Canadian interests.
2. Convergence of American interests.
3. Convergence of European interests.

The convergence of Canadian interests must be
considered without relation to the present or to
those strange political fantasies that appertain to
this generation. It can only be regarded in the
light of historical precedents and those laws that
determine its development as a component part
of the Empire or its transition to a independent
state.

Canada is in an embryonic sense an United States
without its revolution or republicanism. To bring
about in Canada, what occurred a century and a half
ago in the United States only necessitates the exercise of the same means and the portrayal of the
same ignorance to the general principles upon which
depends the perpetuity of the Empire.

The development of Canadian nationalism and
the expansion of Canadian interests cannot be
stopped nor retarded nor circumvented, but must
continue along one of two lines:

THE SAXON AND AMERICA

1. The continuity of the Empire and the continuance of Saxon supremacy.

2. The independance of the Dominion and destruction of Saxon supremacy.

The differentiation between these two ways we have reserved for the latter part of this work, where will be made evident the principles upon which rest the preservation of Saxon Canada, not alone to the Empire, but to herself.

The Canadian Dominion consists of one-sixteenth of the land surface of the globe, and it is in all this vastness that broods the day and deeds of the day we dread to contemplate.

The tendency of Canadian political progression through the character of its people is only determinable by the course of its future population:

(a) Birth-rate of the Saxon population.

(b) Birth-rate of the French population.

(c) British immigration.

(d) American immigration.

(e) European immigration.

As each year increases the facilities of transportation and intercommunication the peoples of the world become more and more mobile. To such a degree has this mobility of races advanced, even at the present time, that in all countries rich in natural resources but deficient in inhabitants the future population consists, not of the descendants of the first inhabitants, but of those nationalities whose source of supply is most abundant and whose mobility is greatest.

With this migration of mankind there goes on in the new land a transmutation of racial ideals. This change, so affecting the ultimate sovereignty of the land, is generally denied, owing to the imperceptibility of its effects—the transient character of the observer and the prejudices that govern his deductions.

When, however, we consider the sources of future population—those nationalities that will eventually people Canada—from the standpoint of British tenure and Saxon domination, we realize its present political relationship and racial supremacy must in due time pass away unless maintained by institutions and power that are removed from without the sphere of the populace, that emanate from and reside in the Saxon race, or, in other words, in the Empire as a whole.

The birth-rate of the present inhabitants of Canada, no matter how great it may be, cannot have any deterrent effect upon those floods that must sooner or later inundate the whole of the Canadian Dominion. The population of unexploited territories has nothing to do, now nor in the future, with localized procreation of mankind. It belongs to his treks, to those new crusades of races wherein the passion that drives them onward is their hungers. Their goal is no longer spiritual; it is the unlooted cupboard of Nature.

The sources of immigration into Canada are the British Isles, Europe, and the United States. In the

United Kingdom alone is to be found a source of immigration that would least affect the continuance of Saxon domination and Imperial unity. The effect of immigration from the United States, on the other hand, reduces Saxon supremacy in proportion as the immigration is non-Saxon. If this is proportionate to the non-Saxon population of the United States, it is between five and seven-twelfths. From a political standpoint American immigration bears in its train the foci of sectional legislation and the precedence of circumscribed environment over national or Imperial considerations. It is the characteristic feature of the American Republic and will change the progression and continuance of Imperial unity to that point of retrocession and deterioration.

While the sources of emigration from the United States is more than twofold, that of the British Isles, that of Europe, is tenfold. In the predominant nationalities now invading Canada there is not to be found a single element that tends to the perpetuation of the Saxon race or that would not destroy its foundations and bring about the final passage of Canadian fealty for the principle of British unity to the control of the non-Saxon elements. The beginning of this is even now apparent in Canadian affairs through the growth of Canadian control over conditions that appertain alone to the Empire. This is due to the development of local politics and consequent subversion of imperialism to sectionalism and the false ideal of equality between the Dominion and the Empire. Equality between the whole and one of its component parts is an impossibility. Canadian interests can possess no such precedence if the Empire is to endure.

What the United States are to-day Canada may be to-morrow. The determination of this transition does not belong primarily to the people of Canada, but to the statesmen of the Empire. As through ignorance of their predecessors the American Colonies were lost to the British nation, in just such a manner may Canada take its departure.

In the loss of the American Colonies the possibility of a Saxon Empire, embracing the entire world, was put aside perhaps forever. There are those who still hold out the delusive hope that, being allies by blood, these two nations may become so politically. This cannot be for two reasons:

1. Whenever one nation is created out of the substance of another by rebellion, there can never exist between the peoples of these two nations mutual confidence and interdependence, for one remains jealous of its old prerogatives and the other of its new.

2. Whenever one nation is created out of the substance of another by rebellion and is subsequently populated by alien races, the alienation becomes two-fold, and to the jealousy of political equality or precedence is added racial antipathy.

That the British Empire and the United States should adhere together in political unity and should establish throughout the world not alone Saxon dominion, but Saxon liberties and principles, is self-evident. But this ideal does not blind us to the improbability of its accomplishment; this is determined by the principles just expressed.

The United States are no longer an Anglo-Saxon nation. With each decade they are drawing farther and farther away from the race of their origin. During the ninety years of immigration only one-fourth of the immigrants have been British. The other three-fourths come from all other quarters of the globe. One-sixth were German, one-twelfth Russian, one-tenth Italian, one-tenth from Austria-Hungary, while the balance has been made up from various other non-Saxon races.

That there should be a declination in British emigration and an increase in that from Europe was inevitable, not only from the disproportion of supply, but from the fact that the British Islands have not only Canada but Australasia and South Africa into which certain of their emigration must flow.

In the last fiscal year the immigration into the United States, exceeding a million of persons, was made up almost entirely of races other than Anglo-Saxon. Eighty-three per cent. of the immigration came from the Mediterranean countries, while the other seventeen per cent. were from various other nations of Europe and Asia. Should this degree of immigration continue for two or three generations, the Anglo-Saxon in America will vanish, racially as well as politically.

Racial supremacy and political intelligence in a nation are diminished as is lengthened the catalogue of its races.

So long as the present sociological conditions continue unchanged in the Republic and its political constitution remains unaltered the nation must, in due time, be given over to those races who can turn up to heaven the greatest number of befouled and stubby noses. The final passage of the American Republic into the control of other races approaches, and with it the Day of the Saxon draws to an end, when the dismalest of twilights shall fall upon it—a twilight that knows no other day.

The political relationship between the United States and the British Empire must be regarded in the same light as that of other alien races. Whatever are their strong wants, these will determine their friendship, no stronger nor weaker than that of other nations. Whenever the angles of their interests become acutely convergent there will be rumors of strife; and when they meet, war will ensue.

In considering the political relationship existent between the British Empire and the Western Hemisphere as a whole and relative to the probabilities of war, we come upon two salient characteristics:

1. That the probabilities of war will increase proportionately as is augmented the political impor-

tance of the hemisphere, its closer contact and inter-relationship with the balance of the world.

2. In the Western Hemisphere the British Empire has to do solely with republics, so that in disputes it has to deal, not with the governments of these nations, but with the multitudes controlling them; not with negotiations that are unmoved by prejudice or self-interest, but with that Cyclopean negotiant itself, whose single flaming eye sees no more than its own wants and into whose dim consciousness only the glow of its own passions penetrates.

Because of these conditions the precipitating causes of war are far in excess of its sources. This condition increases the frequency of war, when, in the natural convergence of international interests, one or both nations are controlled by the populace. It is then difficult to differentiate between the causes and sources of international struggle. In such cases, the lines of national progression rest upon the pivot of a people's passion and ignorance, so that in a single night its natural line of political progress may be altered by those strange trivialities that affect the mob-mind of nations. Its convergence may then become acute, and its movement along a new line of political expansion so rapid that war breaks forth from what mankind is accustomed to call unclouded skies.

These conditions, in themselves so provocative of war, are traceable to one or the other of two distinct causes that concern the British Empire in the wars of the Western Hemisphere—the racial convergence of European interests on this hemisphere.

A nation possesses four degrees of expansion—territorial, economic, political, and racial. These degrees of expansion are in turn dependent not alone upon the potentiality of the expanding state, but also upon the receptive condition of that country toward which its energies are turned. To expand territorially, it must have physical power superior to that of the state whose territories are subject to its expansion. To expand economically it must have a productivity in excess of its own needs and a capacity for the consumption of the resources of other parts of the world. To expand politically, it must possess strong centralization of government and military power greater than the state toward which it is directed plus the military or political protection of its other frontiers. To expand racially is the exodus of the people, due in emigration to the excess of population over the natural resources of the nation; and in immigration due to a reversal of these conditions plus a similarity of climatic conditions and resources to which the expanding race is accustomed. These four conditions determine the relationship of Europe and the Western Hemisphere.

In the period just subsequent to the discovery of America, where the relative military power of the European nations and the aborigines in the New World was so disproportionate, there followed in its natural course the conquest of these undefended continents and the political expansion of European powers. But with the militant decadence of these nations their tenure passed from them, so that, with the exception of the British Empire, only the remnants remain.

The failure of these states to preserve their conquests in the Western Hemisphere was due to five causes:

1. Their militant decline.

2. Their defeat in European wars in which their possessions in the New World were considered as spoils for the victor.

3. The primitive economic condition of that age and the excess of natural resources over the demand.

4. The limited population of Europe, which prevented adequate racial expansion of any or all of these nations.

5. The distance intervening between the Eastern and Western hemispheres as determined by the capacity of transport and the time of communication.

At the present period we find the reverse of these conditions. While the first conquest of the Americas bore only the tentative character of a military expedition and the thievery of kings, it has now changed to the most enduring phase of human conquest—racial expansion. The factors that govern these altered conditions we have already enumerated: the excess of population in Europe over its natural resources, and the reversal of these conditions in the

Western Hemisphere; the similarity of climate and natural products; the elimination of the intervening spaces of sea.

As neither the United States nor Canada has been nor will be solely populated by the reproduction of its original inhabitants, but by immigration, so the settlement of the entire hemisphere must, in due time, be brought about by these same means. And, as the character of this future population is determinable by the quantative supply of its source, the final colonization of the Americans and the determinate factors controlling it are not Saxon, but European or Asiatic.

It is this transfer of European power to the Western Hemisphere in its most durable form, the people themselves, together with their prejudices and institutions, their old hates and hereditary attachments, that must lessen from decade to decade the power of the Saxon over this half of the world.

Heretofore England has established, almost unknown to herself or to the world, a doctrine of American immunity, more real than that enunciated by Monroe, by her control of the Atlantic—a supremacy that was determined not so much by her naval superiority as by maintaining military and political equilibrium among European nations. But now, as the expansion of Europe toward the Western Hemisphere is racial, a new danger is apparent in the domination of the Americas by one or a coalition of European peoples. This will result in the circumscription of the Saxon race and its political elimination in the Western Hemisphere.

As the security of the Empire in the Western Hemisphere is determined by the continuance of military and political equilibrium in Europe, security to the Saxon race in their dominion over the Western Hemisphere is, strange as it may seem, determinable by the same principles.

When a race assumes or attempts to assume dominion over territories greater than the excess of its population can people, or dominates or seeks to dominate races whose population and rate of increase in numbers are greater than its own, it must substitute for its numerical inferiority a degree of military superiority that will increase proportionately with each increment to its dominions and to the numerical increase of the subordinate race.

The invariability of this principle in its application is apparent throughout the history of mankind from the time of his first conquest up to the present, and must continue so long as man is divided into states and races. In ancient times we have the examples of the Macedonian, the Roman, the Moslem, the Mongol; in modern times the Manchu, Spaniard, Frenchman, and Saxon; in the immediate future the Saxon, Teuton, Slav, and Japanese. In ancient times the Roman and the Mongol empires illustrated by the period of their duration the primitive element of the principle that:

1. Inferior numbers plus military capacity results in a sum of actual power.

2. Superior numbers minus military capacity results only in potential power.

The potential power of nations is, contrary to general opinion, of no consequence if the capacity to make use of it for the specific purpose of war is wanting. This potentiality of a nation is inclusive of its people to the same degree as it is of the iron ore in its mountains and other resources of which no use is made for the preparation or conduct of war. Because of this the vastest empires did not disturb the calculations of Alexander nor Mohammed nor Genghis Khan nor Napoleon. The wealth and population of the United States excite no fear in Japan, nor does the vastness of the British Empire cast any foreboding shadow across those routes of march over which Germanic armies expect, in due time, to make their way.

The reverse of these conditions shows the causes that are attendant upon the decline of a military power whenever the numerical inferiority of the conquered nations is very great. After the militant period of conquest is over the declination of militancy in the ruling race proceeds through three channels: racial assimilation, racial deterioration, and militant decadence. This is slow or fast in proportion to the numerical strength of the conquerors and the safeguards they throw around their own race. If the vanquished race possesses a disproportionate excess of population over that of the victors, the conquerors will vanish as soon as did the tribe of Genghis Khan. The declination of militancy in the victor goes on arithmetically while the population of the conquered race increases in geometrical ratio. Though at the time of the conquest each soldier of the victor was equal to fifty or a hundred of the vanquished nation, we soon find that the conquered race is in the ascendant by the natural increase of population and there are two hundred instead of a hundred to one that originally determined their military equality.

4

IV

THE SAXON AND INDIA

Law of National Environment.—Application.—Political Relationship of Empire to Asia.—Loss of India.—Environment of Nature.—Its Effect.—Military Establishment of Nations Over Dependencies.

WHILE the assumption of mankind decreases as his knowledge is added to, the beneficence resulting from this slow erosion of his ignorance is offset by an increase of credulous vanity which often exceeds the increments time makes to his wisdom. That which he formerly assumed as belonging to the gods he now unconcernedly appropriates to himself; he harnesses their powers as Æolus once chained within his cavern the storms of Heaven; he whittles down their thrones into his children's footstools and in their broken temples stalls his reveries and derision.

Yet the mocking truth remains that mankind, even in his aggregates of tribes and nations, has been so circumscribed by his environment that the greatness of his race's destiny has been determined rather by the relative position of its earthy habitat than by the genius of its people or the gods they chose to watch over them.

The Law of National Environment is determinable by three principles:

1. Whenever a physically inferior state is placed between two greater powers so that it is included within their sphere of political and military progression, its independence is never more than tentative and its political survival brief.

2. Whenever a state is surrounded by frontiers that are impregnable through physical conformation, such a state expands no farther than these frontiers and remains externally impregnable, though internally decadent, until the offensive capacity of other nations exceeds its natural defensibility; then it collapses.

3. A state whose political and geographical frontiers are not circumscribed, and whose strategic sphere is alone determinable by the military and political flexibility of its government, continues to progress in power until through military decadence a contraction of its frontiers begins; then it retrogrades.

In the first principle are to be found the factors that determine the extinction of unnumbered nations through all periods of time. The entire history of national life is dimly illumined by the flaring-up of these kingdoms in the wrong and draughty places of the world; their heroic sputterings and goings-out. In these God is of no avail, for Palestine was a state of this description. Valor has nothing to do with their duration, for Poland was such a kingdom. Age adds to them neither sanctity nor protection, for Korea was another country of this misplacement. They belong not alone to the past, but also to the future; and in this tragic category is found Belgium, the Netherlands, Denmark, the Balkans, Persia, and Afghanistan.

Controlled by the conditions of the second principle are to be found fewer states, and they belong entirely to the past, for mankind now recognizes no impregnability in the ramparts, glacis, or moats of nature. Egypt, Peru, Mexico, America, Central Asia, India, China, and Tibet, one after another have they fallen. That impregnability with which nature had shielded them for so many ages and made possible their civilizations also made possible their inevitable collapse when once the persistent ingenuity of mankind broke through the solitudes that surrounded them.

In the third principle alone are to be found the possibilities of supreme racial and world greatness. Operative under it has come up the Saxon race, and concomitant with its rise has taken place that exploration of the world and that development of mechanical means by which it has been accomplished. That the British Empire now encircles the world has been due not so much to the old valor or the old spirit of the race as to the fortuitous circumstance that for the last several centuries the British Islands have been the strategic center of the world. It is now the shifting of this center, or rather the break-ing-up of it into several non-Saxon centers, that constitutes the source of British political disintegration. If it is lost, the supremacy of the Saxon is at an end.

The political relationship of the British Empire to Asia has been in its most salient aspects similar to its relation with America in that it has interposed itself between Europe and Asia in the same manner that it has prevented the political and military expansion of Europe across the Atlantic. This repression of the natural impulse of European political and military expansion in the East as well as in the West is productive of the same sources of war. Only in the precipitating causes that usher in the conflicts is to be found a difference.

Europe can be compared to a vast reservoir filled with constantly expanding matter, and the British Islands the great sluice-gates that regulate the manner of its escapement. There can be no complete repression of Europe within Europe. Whether pacific or violent, this continent must overflow—by emigration so long as the British Empire remains militarily intact, by conquest when the Empire's militancy has fallen away.

England, and not the United States, guarantees the independence of American nations; and in the preservation of the British Empire rather than in the doctrine of Monroe is to be found the basis of their security.

The intervention of the Saxon race between Europe and Asia is also twofold; and, while it has nothing to do with the insidious conquest of immigration, it has to do, on the one hand, with European political and military expansion, and, on the other, with the reversion of Oriental states into the power of their inhabitants.

The political and military relationship of the British Empire to the Far East is reducible to two conditions:

1. The loss or retention of India.

2. The loss or maintenance of the political equilibrium of the Pacific.

Next to a direct attack and seizure of the British Islands the loss of India is the most vital blow that can be given to the Saxon Empire. So closely associated is India with the continuance of the Empire that it is by no means certain—as will be seen later on—that an invasion of England would not be preferable to the conquest of India.

In this consideration the wealth of India plays no part, and though its imports and exports exceed those of the Russian Empire, its population and area are six times greater than those of Germany. Its significance is more portentous than the curtailment of material gains. Its loss means primarily that there has been made in the circle of British dominion a gap so vast that all the blood and fire and iron of the Saxon race cannot again bring together its broken ends.

In the wreck of India is to be found the Golgotha of the Saxon.

While the loss of India may result from two causes

—European conquest or Indian reversion—the retention of India depends upon a single factor—the military supremacy of the Empire, not alone in India, but upon all its frontiers. Hence, while the attack may come from two very different directions, the defense and the preparation for defense are one and the same. To submit to one is to be laid open to both: to be strong against one is to guard against both.

In this chapter will be considered these two causes. Subsequently we will examine in detail their determinate factors and those principles upon which the loss or retention of India depends.

In the relationship that must necessarily exist between a sovereign and a dependent state, two ethical systems are in constant struggle: the ethics of conquest, though the conquest is over; and the ethics of revulsion, though the revolt is not begun. Both are primitive; both are inevitable; both are brutal.

In the development of India under British rule the renascence of Indian nationalism must be the result. Its progress, as in all other subject states governed under similar conditions, is determined by three principles:

1. A primary and slow growth through education and assimilation of the salient characteristics of the sovereign race.

2. A secondary and more rapid progress through the agency of national renascence.

3. Tertiary and sudden florescence through the defeat of the sovereign race upon some other frontier.

With the growth of nationalism in a subject state governed by such laws as are operative in India a renascence of militancy is eventually evolved. This is not due to the fact that a portion of the population are employed as soldiers, by which one might be led to believe that there is infused into them the basic principles of modern military science, but belongs to conditions beyond and outside of this. Ordinarily it might be said that it is the transference to the subject race of those militant qualities that constitutes the dominant character of the conqueror. In the greater part of India, militancy is not the acceptance of something new; it is more: it is the transfiguration of ideals that are as old as the race itself.

It may be a retaliation.

The environment of nature is responsible for this peculiarity in Indian races, as it is for all those fundamental characteristics that differentiate the races of mankind. In Europe, nature and its phenomena, such as would affect primitive man, are relatively insignificant; in India they are appalling. In Europe man has constantly approached the finite; in India he has progressed toward the infinite. In one there has been an increasing indifference to natural forces; in the other a growing consciousness of their illimitability. In one the gods are portrayed with human characteristics; in the other they represent a Himalayan awfulness. In Europe are found Jove with his debaucheries and Jehovah with his prejudices. In India are Siva and Kali, the metamorphosis through the Indian mind of the terrors of his environment, the black abyss of his mountains, his forests and monsters, his seas and storms, his wastes and horrors, and all that is inimical, coercive, and dreadful to man. Out of this came the worship of the terrible and the ethics of fear.

What has this almost primitive condition to do with the British tenure of India? It is the basis of its power. After the Saxon conquered India he destroyed the conditions that made possible the continuance of his tenure without great military power.

Those influences which heretofore controlled and directed the Indian mind were derived from the most sublime and terrible forces in nature. They were remote from man and in comparison only emphasized his feebleness. For man to have assumed a godship in India would have been destructive to the entire system, since no man could inspire that Great Fear which rests alone upon unassailable nature and its phenomena.

The British Empire in its lordship over India must govern by the same conditions. Its rule must be inspired with the same impartiality and grandeur characteristic of nature. The violation of this principle by misgovernment or the defeat of the Empire on another frontier constitutes the basis of hostile militant renascence.

Nothing is more portentous to Saxon power than to inspire the contempt of India.

In regard to the military establishment of nations over dependencies gained by conquest we formulate two general laws, each divisible into two propositions:

1. The military establishment of a nation over a dependency secured by the force of arms can be decreased:

(*a*) After conquest only when the peoples conquered are low in the stage of civilization or few in numbers.

(*b*) When the territory seized is insignificant and possesses no strategic or commercial value to other powers.

2. The military establishment of nations over dependencies gained by conquest must be increased:

(*a*) Proportionately to the increase of nationalism and militancy due to general education and the assimilation of the militant characteristics of the conquerors. This may be rapid or slow, diffused or restricted, and in accordance with these facts must the increase be governed.

(*b*) As the value of the dependency increases either commercially or strategically to one or more nations. This increase must be determined by the acuteness of the angles of their convergent lines of expansion and the rapidity of their movement toward their objective. This rapidity is not measured by any single movement, but by the sum total of that progression which is consecutive and constitutes both natural and predetermined expansion.

The application of these laws to the government of India and the continuance of Saxon tenure needs no commentary.

V

THE SAXON AND INDIA.—*CONTINUED*

Relationship of Population to Landed Area.—Expansion of Races.
—National Boundaries.—Disintegration of a Nation May Begin
on Most Remote Frontier.—Boundaries Militarily Divisible
into Three Classes.—True Sphere of Indian Defense Against
European Advance.

IN national life certain factors affect nations which
are dependent upon the relationship their population bears to the landed area of their habitat and its
productive capacity.   These factors increase in their
intensity when applied to such a nation as India,
where productive expansibility is dependent upon
a corresponding increase in the cultivable land area.
If this addition is not proportionate to the increment of population, then there must result a corresponding change in the productive character of that
increment or a movement of population.

It is not the increase of population in India nor
the character of its employment that has any different military effect there than in other dependent
states subject to the same general conditions.   But
it is the movement of its population, a movement
that will be accelerated as knowledge is diffused
throughout India and as the means of communica-

54

tion with other lands are multiplied, that has a military significance which the Empire cannot ignore.

A modern nation sovereign over alien states has a different task to perform and one that is antithetic to the obligation of former empires. Under present and future conditions governing the interrelationship of sovereign and dependent states, the difference that exists in the political status and civil rights of individuals must continue to grow less and less until they are imperceptibly merged into one common standard. To contend blindly against this natural progression is impossible. What concerns the Saxon is, in granting this personal equality, to maintain the integrity of the Empire and the dominion of the race.

We have heretofore stated as an axiom that in an empire made up of heterogeneous racial elements it can only endure so long as the military power and governmental direction remain in the hands of a homogeneous people. But to this principle it is necessary to add the corollary that the ruling race cannot, without disintegrating effects, fail to realize that progression is not confined to them alone; and preparation for the territorial expansion of such dependencies as India must be proportionate to their development.

It is necessary to consider only one phase of this principle as applicable to the movement of Indian population and the increased military responsibility it involves. Notwithstanding that India is the second greatest nation in the world in point of population—fifth as regards wealth—and possesses to a corresponding degree all the elements of national and racial expansion, no provision has been made for this overflow; but, on the contrary, legislation has attempted, in the blindest manner, the impossible task of its curtailment. While India is as much a part of the British Empire as South Africa, Australia, or Canada, yet British Indian subjects are prohibited from domicile in these dominions, though part of a common Empire.

Of the many phases in military progression that such legislation gives expression to, we are now concerned with:

1. The Empire's duty to India in providing for its natural expansion.

2. Its duty to the dominions in recognizing the justice of their contention that racial amalgamation is impossible.

Without this amalgam, unity can only be found in segregation.

The expansion of races is more or less controlled by natural laws less applicable in modern times than in former ages. With each advance of civilization these natural factors become less and less potent. But we find that the great and little movements of people still follow certain inherent laws, one of which is that they move along not longitudinal but latitudinal lines, and the habitat they eventually establish as they trek these old unmarked highways of the world is determined by a certain similitude of climatic and other natural conditions to which, racially, they had long been accustomed. As determined by these conditions, we find two natural lines of Indian racial and territorial expansion that are far removed from those dominions inhabited by white races:

1. The Aryan races in Northern India should move westward to Asia Minor.

2. The non-Aryan races should move eastward to the East Indies.

This territorial expansion of India, including Persia and Asia Minor on the west, Burma, the Malay Peninsula, and the Indies on the east, is in its final analysis politically correct, provided that it does not go beyond nor stop short of those lands that constitute the true frontiers of India.

It is in the study of these strategic lines that we discover this territorial expansion of India to be, in its extreme, not only confined within the true strategic frontiers, but until this territorial expansion is accomplished, tentatively or otherwise, it can be said that the Indian Empire, contracted within a sphere remote from its real frontiers, is deprived of its first essentials of defense.

Modern life has produced many anomalies in the interrelationship of states. We see, more and more, the substitution of human ordinances for natural laws and the constant increase in the belief that they are imperishable. Yet they are as vain and futile as those fantasies that lay out the architecture of Heaven toward which solemn millions move in confidence. To these delusions we find, in modern times, a counterpart in the chimeras of statesmen—or, more correctly speaking, in those who should be statesmen, but who nevertheless lead on their nations to the same small gateway beyond which all illusions vanish and all hope to correct the errors of humanity is put aside.

Of the present delusions that are now leading mankind upon those blind trails that end nowhere the two most characteristic are those of Universal Peace and the delimitation of national boundaries.

All national frontiers are subject to constant fluctuation and must be forever shrinking or expanding. They can no more remain delimited than can the coast-line of oceans, for they are those indefinable shores where break the restless, turbulent seas of life.

Of the several principles governing the movement of national boundaries we are alone concerned with those that affect India: first, as regards its own integrity and progression: secondly, the relation its frontiers bear to the solidarity and continuance of the Empire. These are reducible to three principles:

1. The frontiers of India coincide with those of the United Kingdom in exact proportion as their violability affects the integrity of the Empire.

2. Permanency of the present Indian frontiers is only possible through:

(*a*) Stationary or lessening population.

(*b*) Repression of Indian political and economic development.

(*c*) Voluntary retrocession before the expansion of Germany, Russia, and Japan.

3. The expansion of the present Indian frontiers is made inevitable by:

(*a*) Increasing population.

(*b*) Economic and political development.

(*c*) Territorial expansion of Germany, Russia, and Japan, convergent upon India or its interests.

(*d*) The military necessity of a new alignment of Indian frontiers.

That the first principle should appear anomalous is to be expected, though the paradox is, in reality, the failure to recognize its truth. Mankind is too apt to forget that, as the character of national life alters, international relationship must undergo a change. It does not occur to him that the frontiers of maritime empires are, in their military and political significance, totally different from those frontiers belonging to states whose territories are homogeneous and integral. Moreover, we seldom find that any distinction is made between those factors that adjusted the frontiers of ancient maritime empires and those that are decisive under modern conditions.

Interdependence in the defense of frontiers increases proportionately as is increased their intercommunicability with the military centers of both the offense and the defense.

In former times each frontier was self-contained, and its defense or loss was by no means dependent upon the security of remote boundaries, especially those of oversea possessions. But in modern times these conditions have all been changed, and the duration of national life is no longer dependent upon the security of a capital. The disintegration of the greatest nation may begin upon its most remote frontiers. So when we say that the frontiers of India coincide with those of the United Kingdom, we mean that their violation will have, in due time, the same effect upon the continuance and solidarity of the Empire as an attack upon the British Isles. A complete exemplification of this principle has been deferred to a subsequent chapter of this volume.

The propositions contained in the second and third principles are self-evident, except the last two, which deal with: (1) the territorial expansion of Germany, Russia, and Japan in their convergence upon India and its interests; (2) the consequent realignment of Indian frontiers.

The territorial expansion of Germany, Russia, and Japan, the basic principles upon which their expansion is founded, the degree of its propulsion, and the effect as regards not alone India but the entire Empire will be examined into in a future portion of this work. For the present we will consider tentatively how this has brought about the necessity of a new adjustment of the Indian frontiers.

It is believed that when there is an advance against the frontiers of a nation the best policy is either the strengthening of the existent lines or a contraction of them. The reasons for such a belief are evident. As many others, they are founded on conditions no longer vital. They are not applicable to the frontiers of India.

The boundaries of nations in a military sense are divisible in three classes and are subject to a like number of military distinctions in their defense:

1. When the frontiers are contiguous with those of a more powerful military state.

2. When the frontiers are contiguous with those of a weaker military state.

3. When the frontiers are contiguous with those of a decadent state, intervening between the aggressive and defensive states.

In the first condition we are confronted with a purely military defensive which may only be served by the strengthening of existing frontiers, or, if strategic conditions warrant and the internal weakness of the state demand it, by their contraction.

In the second condition we find a purely offensive movement, with the expansion of national boundaries which will be temporary or permanent as the conclusion of the war determines.

India, however, is only concerned with the third condition, which has heretofore received little or no consideration in military science. We, therefore, lay down this axiom: that when the frontiers of a nation are contiguous to those of a militarily decadent state, intervening between it and a convergent power, then that decadent state, or such portions of it as determined by strategic considerations, must be occupied, tentatively or otherwise, as soon as the intention of the aggressive state is ascertained.

We have shown that whenever an inferior state is placed within the military sphere of two great powers at war, it ceases to possess those international rights that are supposed to go with neutrality. When, moreover, such a state directly intervenes between the frontiers of two warring powers, it becomes in the beginning of hostilities the theater of combat and is subject to the maximum hardship of war, since, belonging to neither combatant, it receives the protection of neither and is, in a sense, the enemy of both.

When such a condition exists, the power which is able to seize, prior to war, the extreme frontier of the buffer state secures an advantage. It is because of this determinate factor that whenever it is apparent that the expansion of a rival power is convergent upon one or more of the Empire's frontiers, then that frontier, instead of contracting or retaining its alignment, should, if conditions permit, be pushed forward in direction of the territorial advance of the hostile power. Those spheres of influence which the great powers have marked out for themselves in different parts of the world are valuable or are, on the other hand, a source of weakness. This depends upon their location and utilization in accordance with these principles.

There are in the world only three countries that possess pre-eminent strategic positions: the British Islands, the Japanese Islands, and India. The Indian Empire is in the strategic center of the third most important portion of the globe. Its influence has had its effect upon the European mind from the earliest times; and in the future the power of its strategic position as a determinate factor in world politics will increase with each international readjustment.

It is, however, the corelationship of British possessions in the Indian and Pacific oceans, in Africa and Asia Minor, that gives to India, as the center of this vast region, its unique greatness and power. Radiating from it as a center, with one vortex common to all, are thirteen strategic triangles surrounding the entire Indian sphere.[1] These are divisible into two classes: those confined to British territory and those that are not. Eleven of these triangles belong to the former and two to the latter class. The first are the result of acting in strict accordance with the laws of political and military strategy, and give, in their offensive and defensive capacity, complete security to those regions over which their spheres extend. Westward they include Arabia

[1] Chart I.

and the east coast of Africa from Aden to Cape Town. Southward they include the entire Indian Ocean; southeast, Australia and New Zealand; eastward the Malay Peninsula and the Straits Settlements.

These eleven strategic triangles have outside of India three subsidiary centers: Asia Minor, the center of the western sphere; the triangle Seychelles, Mauritius, Diego Garcia, the center of the southern sphere; and Singapore, the center of the eastern. The corelation and interdependence of these centers on India show clearly the truth of the statement that India constitutes the principal strategic center of this portion of the world and that with its loss there must fall away simultaneously all this vast region over which the Saxon now rules.

As we thus contemplate India apparently invulnerable, in the very center of her strategic environs, it seems impossible to conjecture her invasion or conquest. But almost in the same manner as the heel of Achilles was always with him, so there exists in every system of defense and in every empire some point of vulnerability. India has this point. And, anomalous as it may appear, the point of greatest danger, unlike the god's heel, is the one most exposed and toward which the expansion of the two greatest military powers in the world are convergent—the northwest frontier of India.

Two strategic triangles constitute the true sphere of Indian defense against European advance:

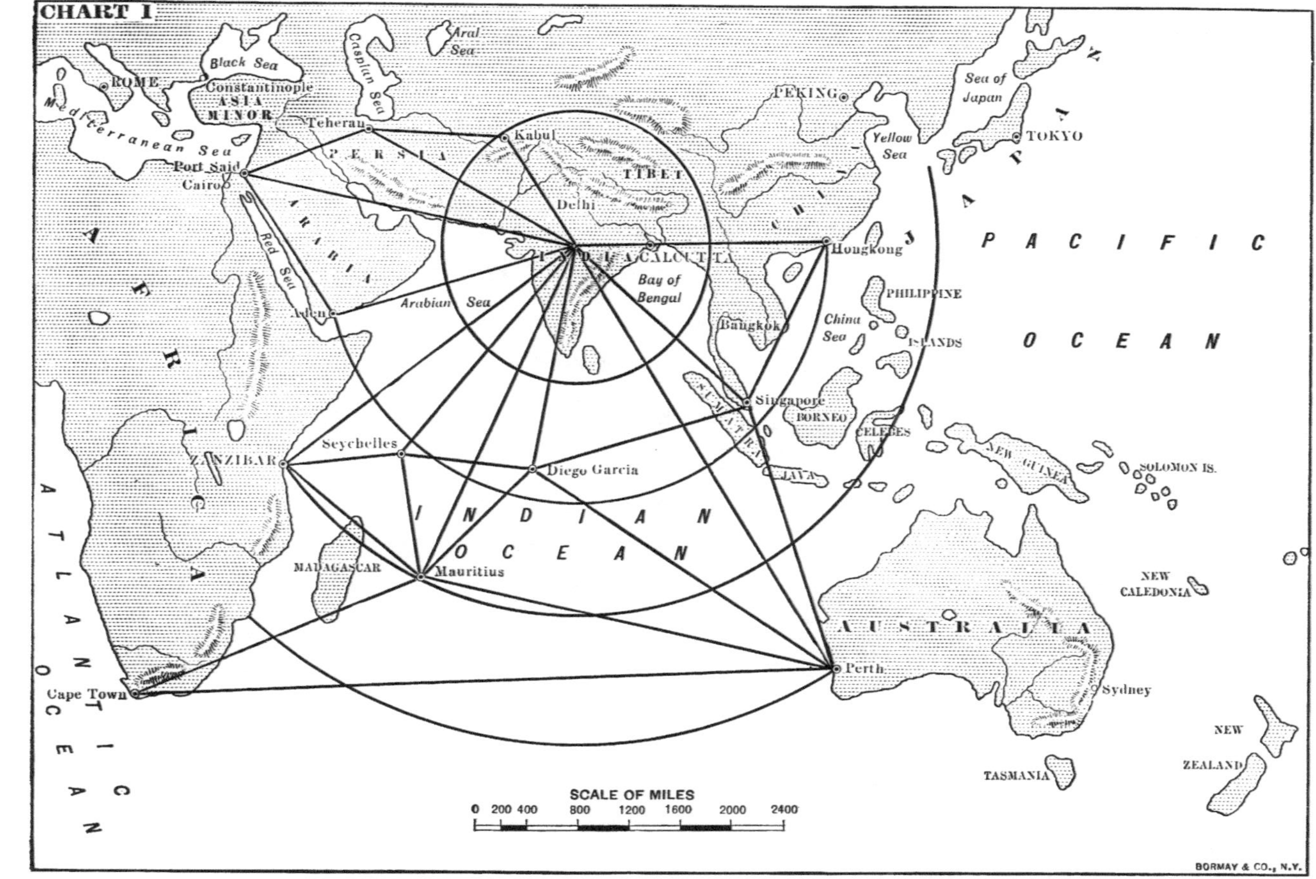

CHART I
Mediterranean Sea
ROME
Black Sea
Constantinople
ASIA MINOR
Caspian Sea
Aral Sea
PEKING
Sea of Japan
TOKYO
Teheran
Kabul
TIBET
Yellow Sea
JAPAN
Port Said
Cairo
PERSIA
Delhi
PACIFIC
OCEAN
Red Sea
ARABIA
INDIA CALCUTTA
Hongkong
CHINA
Aden
Arabian Sea
Bay of Bengal
Bangkok
China Sea
PHILIPPINE ISLANDS
AFRICA
Singapore
SUMATRA
BORNEO
CELEBES
NEW GUINEA
SOLOMON IS.
Seychelles
Diego Garcia
JAVA
ZANZIBAR
INDIAN
OCEAN
NEW CALEDONIA
MADAGASCAR
Mauritius
AUSTRALIA
NEW
ATLANTIC
Perth
Sydney
Cape Town
OCEAN
TASMANIA
NEW ZEALAND
SCALE OF MILES
0 200 400 800 1200 1600 2000 2400
BORMAY & CO., N.Y.

THE SAXON AND INDIA

1. The triangle India, Kabul, Teheran—against Russian advance.

2. The triangle India, Port Said, Teheran—against German advance.

Russia should not be permitted to pass the line Kabul-Teheran nor Germany the line Port Said-Teheran. By this it is seen that Persia is, equally with India, common to both triangles and, constituting the center of these two tentative frontiers, is the key to the defense of India from European aggression.

VI

THE SAXON AND THE PACIFIC

Importance of India in Defense of Australasia.—Relation of Brown and Yellow Races to.—Movement of Asian Population toward.— Home Defense Impossible. — Australasia Insular. — Australia Divided into Seven Military Spheres.—Seizure Restricted to Two.

THE general tendency to regard the various phenomena of existence in an intrinsic sense is productive of much error, since in life nothing exists alone. As an individual is only a partial analysis of humanity, so a nation is only a partial synthesis. Because of this the source of greatness in nations, as well as in individuals, is always relative, and sometimes is so inherent in external conditions as to be entirely removed from those factors upon which we ordinarily base our ideas of power and sovereignty.

This is true of India.

The great error of England is its ignorance of India. By this is not meant ignorance in internal government or economies, but in a just recognition of its political relationship with the world and in its character as the basis of the British Empire.

The real greatness of India might be said to be

without itself, yet belonging to it much in the same manner as the greatness of kings is in the totality of their monarchy.

Had India not been where it is there would have resulted no British Empire.

Only because India is British are the Mediterranean and Red seas, Malta, Cyprus, Egypt, the Suez, and coasts of Asia Minor under Saxon sovereignty. For the same reason Africa is principally British as well as Mauritius, Seychelles, and other islands of the Indian Ocean together with Burma, the Straits Settlements, Hongkong, New Zealand, and Australia.

Were it not for India the British nation would have been confined to the United Kingdom and America.

It was India that brought the Saxon eastward, and it was the strategic position of India[1] that made possible their Empire.

India, in a military sense, is the Empire, and only so long as Saxon dominion over it continues unbroken and its frontiers remain inviolate will it be possible for the British Empire to endure.

The second factor that governs the interrelationship of the Empire and the Orient is restricted to the loss or maintenance of the political and military equilibrium of the Pacific. This factor is subordinate, in both its political and military character, to that of India, since such equilibrium in

[1] Chart I.

the Pacific is primarily dependent upon the loss or retention of that country. But there are conditions toward which the Empire is now tending that may so destroy this equilibrium that it will result in the eventual loss of India and the consequent disintegration of the Empire.

This question of the Pacific is restricted to two phases:

1. The relation of British Pacific dominions to the Empire and Asian nations.

2. The relation of the Empire to its Pacific dominions and Asian nations.

Contrary as it is to general opinion, mankind's cognition of his progression succeeds rather than precedes his development and those successive changes he undergoes. Mankind belongs to the progeny of Epimetheus.

In modern times this condition is apparent in the persistence with which some nations remain blind to the ever-changing character of their international association, altering to a greater or less degree each time the earth completes its orbit. Those conditions most vital to the existence and greatness of nations are first affected. This rigidity of human ignorance increases in direct ratio as is augmented the control of the populace over the affairs of state.

Because of these swiftly shifting phases of modern life the military relationship of the United States to both Europe and Asia has entirely changed within a single generation; yet public opinion has not altered, and that nation has been reduced to a defense-less condition proportionately as old facts have become modern delusions and those old truths new lies.

The people of Australia and New Zealand, in consideration of their control of public affairs, are no exception to the above rule, and they have shown no greater prescience than the people of the United States in regard to the new military interrelationship of nations and its inherent dangers. Australasia has stopped short of what it wishes to accomplish—the preservation of their possessions to the Saxon race.

The security of Australasia rests entirely upon one condition — the integrity and continuance of the British Empire. Concomitant with its defeat and disintegration Saxon dominion in the south Pacific comes to an end. As we have seen that even if Canada should become independent or American, Africa Dutch or independent, the Empire might continue; but with the loss of India through revolt or conquest the Empire is shattered and Saxon Australasia will at that time, or in the final political and military readjustment of the Pacific, pass under the tenure of another race.

The first principle of Australasian defense is the defense of India.

While it is impossible to look ahead and determine with exactitude the futurity of nations, yet it is possible to approximate, by the concurrence and general drift of international activity, the events of the immediate future; and upon this approximation consider, under different sets of given circumstances, probabilities more distant. The future of Australasia is illustrative of this truth.

It can be regarded in modern times as a basic principle that whenever a rich and sparsely inhabited region lies within the sphere of the racial expansion of greater and more populous empires, that expansion will result unless prohibited by potential or actual power superior to that of the expanding race. Moreover, we find that the power made use of in the original prohibition cannot remain fixed, but must be increased proportionately as is increased the power of the expanding nations plus their augmented proximity as determined by modern transportation. The relation of Saxon Australasia to the brown and yellow races of Asia is productive of two portentous factors:

1. Australasia is nearly as large as Europe, while its population is less than that of the city of London.

2. Surrounding Australasia are Asian empires with a population approximately three times greater than that of Europe.

The period when a race's natural expansion becomes migratory is determined when the population exceeds the productive capacity of their native soil plus the knowledge and ability to reach those lands that give to their labor not alone sustenance but increment.

THE SAXON AND THE PACIFIC

At some more or less definite time, which may or may not be the present, the natural movement toward Australasia by Asia will begin. There are two tentative preventions, one peaceful, the other military. The first by populating these regions with Saxons or white races. Second by military power enforcing the prohibition of Asian immigration. The impossibility of the first prohibitory measure is apparent, since the increase of the Saxon population must go on in the future, as in the past, by propagation and voluntary immigration. Yet the relative disproportion in numerical strength now existing between the white races of Australasia and the colored races of Asia will not decrease, but will, on the other hand, be augmented in a constantly increasing ratio, for there is in this dual propagation another strange fatality.

While eighty years are necessary for the white race, under the best of conditions, to double its numbers, the brown and yellow races under the worst conditions double theirs in one-fourth less time. To have confidence, therefore, in the ability of the Saxons to preserve to themselves through immigration or propagation Australasia and its environs is only expressive of futility. In this belief is found the apocalypse of the white man's ignorance.

We are now reduced, in the retention of Saxon sovereignty over Australasia, to the single principle of military defense, but a defense in its conception and use far different from that now practised through-out these Pacific dominions.

The vast numerical superiority of the brown and yellow races over the white in the Pacific and Indian oceans has its corollary in the modern combative equality of all races. The universality of knowledge, and a similar universality in the application of science, places all of mankind on an equal footing as regards the use of mechanical appliances in war or in the business of peace. With the establishment of equality in the means of conducting war we must revert for its decision to that old factor, the inequality of population and the numerical disproportion between the forces engaged. It is in this realization that the armaments and military knowledge of Asian empires are now equal to those of Australasia that we become cognizant of the ominous gulf that separates the six millions of Saxons in the south Pacific from the thousand millions that surround them.

Upon the cognition of these facts alone must the defense of Australasia be based. In other words, home defense for Australasia and New Zealand is a military anomaly. The frontiers of Australasia are remote from the south Pacific. They have no fixity. They shift from one quarter of the empire to another, constantly changing, but invariably coinciding with those portions of the empire against which an attack is being directed. The universality of Australasian frontiers is due to their inherent necessity of being imperial. The normal position of Australasia in the defense of the Empire is the defense of India.

While the Pacific colonies and dominions can never possess alone that defensive capacity sufficient to prevent the seizure of their territories by any power which has gained control of their seas, yet they constitute a source of war and become more constantly provocative of it as the Pacific becomes more and more the foci of human struggle.

The time has passed forever when a relatively small community possessing a vast area of undeveloped wealth can secure this to themselves in that illusive freedom mankind calls independence. When now, and more so in the future, a colony or dominion passes without the protective sphere of a great power, either through imperial disintegration or by secession, it lingers but a moment in the mirage of its delusive sovereignty, then passes into the keeping of another empire whose internal expansion constitutes the *motif* to its conquest.

It was this tentative independence, already noticed, that lost to the Transvaal and Orange Free State their character as distinct political entities. Coming within the sphere of Imperial progression, their absorption was predetermined so long as they were not a portion of another nation as strong or stronger than the British Empire. If Australia and New Zealand were sovereign nations, their relations to Asian empires would be no different from that of the African states to the British nation, except in the degree of intensity which controls the impulse of Asian expansion. Over this expansion Australasia alone could have no control. It could neither threaten nor circumvent.

Each day the world grows smaller; each day mankind is being more crowded and jostled together. In this universal pressure all is in a state of flux— man and his habitat. Because of this, decadent and minor states must gravitate with increasing momentum toward the larger and more powerful nations. Because of this Australasia is dragging closer and closer to the shores of Asia. Yet it is not war that is doing this; it is peace: not the conquests of kings, but the hungers of their subjects; not man in his elementary character of marauder, but man in his highest civilization, in his ten thousand new necessities — his speech across the waters, his flight across the seas.

Australasia is not fixed, in the sense of racial or national security, upon the bed of its ocean. It is fixed only so long as it is anchored to the British Empire. Whenever these chains are broken it is adrift like a derelict upon a sea of storm.

In this work only those basic principles governing the defense of Australasia concern us. For if once these principles are understood, and all military preparations based upon them, the errors and misconceptions that must creep in and constitute a definite portion of their detail are immaterial. But if the foundations upon which are erected the defense of these dominions are false, then there can be no superstructure regardless of the labor expended but will prove to be worthless. It is because of this fact that the efforts now being made for Australasian defense are so delimited that they form an immaterial factor in the ultimate struggle for national survival. They belong to world conditions that no longer exist.

The defense of a country and the manner of its execution are determined by two principal factors:

1. The direction from which the attack is to come.

2. The character of the nation's geographical environment.

The defense of Germany against Russia is entirely different from that which would be employed against England. So, in the geographical environment, the manner of defense varies. An insular nation is subject to conditions that have little or nothing to do with those wars waged between two continental states. The preparation for these two distinct classes of war must vary accordingly, although nations cannot be confined strictly to these two distinctions. Austria, Turkey, Russia, and China are continental nations. England and Japan are insular. Still we find that there are other continental states that also possess, in one form or another, certain characteristics of insular powers, as Germany, France, and the United States. On the other hand, the British Empire in India and elsewhere and Japan in Korea and Manchuria are subject to the same responsibilities as continental countries. In most modern nations, therefore, we find that, in so far as their military preparation is concerned, there must always be maintained a flexible equilibrium between their naval and military preparations, governed in their variability by the direction from which the attack is to come or by the necessities attendant upon their expansion.

Had Japan, although an insular state, possessed her naval development alone and neglected her land forces, the war against Russia would have failed. But, recognizing the true principle of flexibility in military preparation, Japan adopted against a continental power its characteristics of continental warfare.

Considering Australasia as a sovereign nation, with its inherent military responsibilities, what constitutes the error of its defense? It is in the adoption of a continental system to the protection of insular territory. While both Japan and Great Britain are insular kingdoms, they are not without continental attributes; but, as regards Australasia, it is, in the widest sense of the term, wholly insular, and does not possess one single characteristic of a continental power that would justify the illusion of home defense in the sense now understood.

Australasia lies apart from the balance of the world. It is a continent of its own in its own vast hemisphere of water. Its plants and animals are not those of the Old or the New World; but are peculiar to that vast isolation nature could not overcome. Only within the last two generations man has succeeded where nature failed.

A narrow channel alone separates the United Kingdom from Europe; between Japan and Asia are the tragic Straits of Tsu Shima; but beyond the shores of Australasia are two oceans: Cape Town six thousand miles away, North America nearly seven, and, while Asia is less than four thousand, the United Kingdom is more than twelve. It is this almost illimitable isolation that constitutes Australasia's purely insular character.

The permanent defense of Australasia is naval.

Its land forces, if adequate, can assure that defense of its shores only if the control of the sea by the enemy is temporary; but if the maritime supremacy is undisturbed or permanent, the defense can only last for a relatively short time.

This is determined by three conditions:

1. The relative disproportion between the attacking forces and the defenders:

 (*a*) Disparity in population and wealth between Australasia and the power capable of attack.

 (*b*) Australasia is divided into seven distinct military spheres that are neither corelative nor co-operative.

 (*c*) The defense of the whole is determined

by the struggle of the strongest sphere, the population of this region determining the defensive potentiality of the whole.

2. Nine-tenths of the population live adjacent to the sea.

3. Retreating inland, instead of moving toward the base of their resources, they move away from them with the first retrograde movement.

The seven military spheres[1] of Australia are: (1) the environs of Perth on the west coast; (2) the environs of Adelaide and (3) Melbourne on the south coast; (4) the environs of Sydney and (5) Brisbane on the east coast, together with the two islands of New Zealand. It is seen[1] that Western Australia has, in a military sense, no defensive interrelationship with the other six spheres because of its isolation. All its efforts will be restricted to its own sphere.

This is also true of the two New Zealand spheres, while the same isolation exists between the remaining four spheres whenever (1) the line of railway between Adelaide and Brisbane is broken, or (2) by the voluntary segregation of those spheres enforced by the freedom of the enemy's movements.

Any concentration of all the forces into one sphere results in the unhindered occupation of the other six. So decisive are the determinate conditions of the geography of Australia in favor of the invader that any such concentration will result

[1] Chart II.

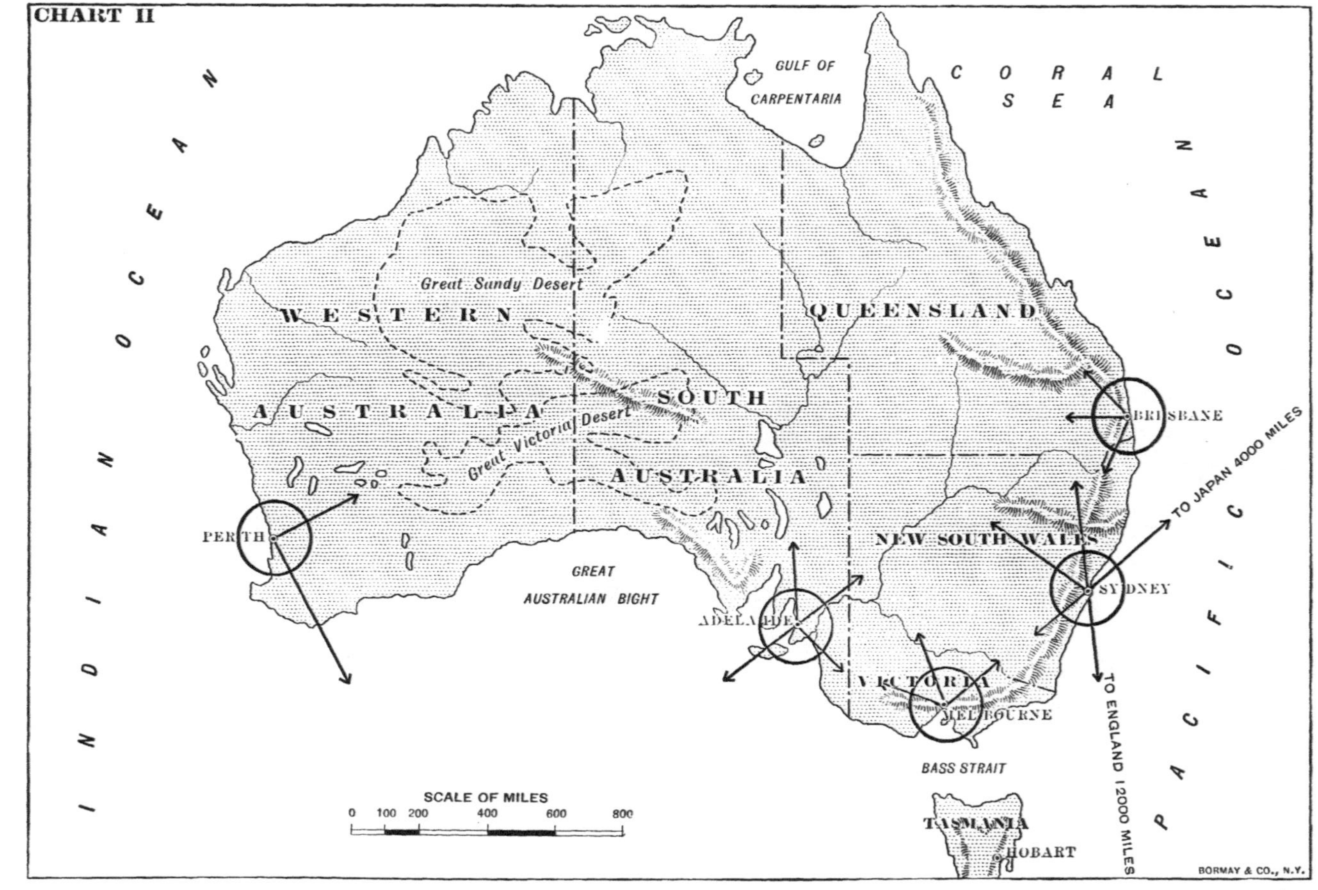

CHART II
INDIAN OCEAN
PERTH
WESTERN AUSTRALIA
Great Sandy Desert
Great Victoria Desert
SOUTH AUSTRALIA
GREAT AUSTRALIAN BIGHT
QUEENSLAND
GULF OF CARPENTARIA
ADELAIDE
VICTORIA
MELBOURNE
NEW SOUTH WALES
SYDNEY
BRISBANE
BASS STRAIT
TASMANIA
HOBART
TO ENGLAND 12000 MILES
TO JAPAN 4000 MILES
CORAL SEA
PACIFIC OCEAN
SCALE OF MILES
0 100 200 400 600 800
BORMAY & CO., N.Y.

in the capitulation of the defense. If, on the other hand, not knowing where the attack is to fall, military activity is restricted to the purely home defense of these respective spheres, we are compelled to witness by a single movement of the invading force their complete isolation and destruction in detail.

The seizure of Australasia is primarily restricted to two strategic spheres: [1]

1. The New South Wales sphere, the city of Sydney being the base. This base constitutes the arc of invasion.

2. The Victoria sphere, Melbourne being the center of the arc of invasion.

As will be apparent later, these two strategic spheres constitute the defensive area of entire Australasia.

The second condition that is preventive of protracted Australasian land defense, without ultimate naval succor, is due to the fact that nine-tenths of the Australasian population live adjacent to the seaboard. More than that, they are concentrated into the five spheres[1] already considered. Approximately half of the population of Western Australia is dependent upon the Perth sphere; three-fourths of of South Australia are constrained within the Adelaide sphere; while two-fifths of the state of Victoria are confined to the city of Melbourne; in New South Wales over half the population is re-

[1] Chart II.

stricted to the Sydney sphere; the same is approximately true of the Brisbane region in Queensland.

It is this fatality, the restriction of Australia's population to coast regions, that is the determinate factor in the impossibility of prolonged land defense against a nation in control of the ocean. The seaboard population of Australia is, in a military sense, very different from that of other countries. It is not alone the beginning of the state's population; it is the beginning and the end. Australia, while a continent, is also an atoll; without the ocean, within the desert. Both the sea and the desert are, as regards military calculations, identical. To retreat toward the ocean in control of the enemy is disaster; to flee to the desert is death.

The land defense of Australia against invasion is the antithesis of any other modern state exposed to invasion from the sea. Ordinarily, in the defense of sea frontiers, each retrograde movement should be concentric and toward the wealth and population centers of the nation. But in the case of Australia there could be no retrograde movement that would be concentric and toward a common base. There is no main base. Each sphere possesses its own, not distant from, but in the center of, its theater of hostilities. So delimited and segregated are these spheres that the retreat of a single week puts the defense beyond the means of waging war.

Once the defense of eastern Australia is thrown westward of the Blue Mountains, and the defense of southern Australia is pushed north of the Australian Alps, organized defense in the form of armies will pass into that final stage of inutile warfare, guerrilla and predatory, until, self‑exhausted, it reaches its end.

What nature gave the Boors it has denied Australia.

The defense of Australasia is the defense of Australia, and is divisible into two parts:

1. The temporary defense depends upon land forces whose numbers, owing to the segregation of its defensive spheres, must be equal in each sphere to the probable force of the enemy's invading armies. Australian defensive forces must not be considered in the aggregate. Their maximum defensive capacity is never greater than that of the strongest single sphere.

The character, armament, and training of Australian forces are determinable, not by Australian legislation, but by the character, armament, and training of the strongest probable enemy.

2. The permanent defense of Australasia is naval, the strength of which is determined by the maximum naval capacity of the strongest maritime power capable of attack.

This degree of naval power can never be attained by Australasia.

It is possible only to a unified British Empire.

VII

THE SAXON AND EASTERN ASIA

Principle on Which National Activities Must be Based.—Empire Must be Defended as a Whole.—Danger to a Nation in Concentrating Defense to One Frontier. — International Alliances.— Equilibrium in Pacific.—Expansion of China.—Effect of Russian Defeat by Japan.

WE will later continue the conclusions of Australasian defense. Our present purpose is only to show the essentials of Imperial progression and the dependence of Australia upon its solidarity: to right the errors of their former conceptions and make plain that, in the preservation of their Saxon ideals, they have set out upon a way that leads from instead of toward their consummation.

There is but one principle upon which must be based all of their national activities and toward which all of their aspirations must be directed—the principle of Imperial solidarity. Likewise, there is but a single truth to guide them, the very opposite of the delusion that now holds sway over their minds— the truth that their survival as a state belongs not to themselves, but to their race, to the continuance and progression of the Empire.

In the interdependability of the various parts of

82

the Empire, and for the defense of their respective regions, there must be determined a definite interchangeability of the means, a definite place and predetermined plan for each division of the Empire upon the never-ending battle-fields of the world.

While Australasia possesses for its own preservation those obligations toward Imperial defense which we have already considered, the Empire, in turn for its preservation, possesses equivalent obligations toward the defense of Australasia.

It must be regarded as an inviolable principle that any loss of territory reacts upon the Empire, the fatality of which is in direct ratio to the political importance of the region lost. In the government of a maritime empire it can be considered as axiomatic that the loss of previously acquired political and territorial rights, or even the tendency to acquiesce in any such loss, is indicative of national retrocession and Imperial decadence.

The difference in effect of Imperial defeat to Australasia and the loss of Australasia to the Empire is only that of time. Imperial disintegration results in the immediate end of Saxon Australasia. On the other hand, the loss of so large a portion of the Empire as Australasia is the beginning of Imperial disintegration, since the causes productive of the loss are the results of nothing more nor less than a corresponding degree of Imperial weakness.

The most dangerous belief that ever laid hold of

the Saxon race is the delusion that by defending separately their segregated portions of the Empire they are able to defend the whole; whereas it is only true that by the defense of the Empire, in its concrete character, are the components protected.

While Australasia has not provided for its proportionate obligation in the defense of the Empire, the Imperial obligations toward the commonwealth have not been met to any greater degree. There is a salient difference between the obligations of the dominions and those of the Empire. The former are simple, the latter complex. Hence it can be said that to the degree that this complexity exists are the Imperial responsibilities increased. So involved are these responsibilities that, unless there exists a singleness of purpose in Imperial policy, those very expedients made use of as protective measures may in turn become the source of many dangers.

The defense of a nation or its dependencies does not always involve the use of force. Statesmen defend and lose greater interests than soldiers, and it is more generally upon their wisdom or ignorance that national greatness or survival depends. Wars result from the maximum of their intelligence, which is national growth, and from the maximum of their ignorance, which is national retrocession.

The failure of the Imperial government, in the discharge of its obligations to the Pacific dominions and colonies, has been due to a false differentiation of the Empire's political and military development in the two hemispheres. This progress should not be erratic, but should be governed in its development by well-defined laws. It is only the shifting interests of men, and the transitory character of their expedients in the government of the Empire, that give to its military and political expansion that lack of unity and cohesion that should mark its progress.

It was this undue concentration of Louis XIV. and Napoleon upon continental affairs that, blinding them to the potentiality of a sea power, brought about their downfall. It was this same delimitation of Russia's horizon that, in the vastness of China, Japan was not apparent. In the same manner England's concentration against France and Russia permitted the birth and the maturity of the German menace. And now, while the attention of the whole Empire is directed toward this most apparent peril, Russia is still moving along her predetermined way.

In the Pacific, scorned by Saxon vanity or denied by Saxon ignorance, broods a new peril in a kind of sullen gentleness not unlike the typhoon that also, in these purple solitudes, awaits those who forget.

It is not always potent reasons that force the attention of nations upon a single frontier to the neglect of the others. This is more apt to happen through the most trivial occurrences. Like the mariners of antiquity, nations crowd their fears toward the barkings of Scylla while being sucked into the whirlpools of Charybdis.

In the philosophy of nation-building we are at first confronted with such a complexity of apparent principles that it appears an almost impossible labor to burrow down to those basic conditions, few in number, yet the determinate factors of political life.

The peculiarity of life is its ultimate simplicity.

The building-up of an empire and its preservation is reducible to two principles:

1. The use of the militant power of the nation itself.

2. The use or neutralization of the militant power of other nations.

The latter, which alone concerns us at present, is generally exemplified in international alliances. The essential characteristic of national defense or expansion based upon alliances is the increase of national strength, either negatively, by neutralizing the enemy's military power, or positively, by destroying it.

International alliances should be governed by three elemental conditions:

1. An alliance should not be made with a state that increases the probabilities of war and augments through war the power of that nation with whom the alliance is made.

2. No alliance is permissible between nations whose lines of expansion and interests are acutely convergent.

3. That in the event of a successful war the allied power will not gain by its victory such political power and strategic position as to encroach upon the political and economic sphere of its ally.

It is objected, when the error of an alliance becomes apparent, that the ultimate consequences of such compacts are unable to be determined. This is wrong. Alliances are made in peace for the purposes of war; and, being made prior to war, the conditions governing their association extend no further than the war. The conditions resultant from war, whether victorious or otherwise, should constitute the decisive factors in the formation of the alliance.

It was this indifference to future consequences that led the Empire into the Japanese Alliance, creating the third most potent factor in those forces which tend to bring about the dissolution of the Empire. While, on the other hand, the purpose for which this alliance was made has, as will be shown later, increased the very dangers which the alliance endeavored to modify.

The policy of opposing an Oriental power against European advance in Asia is correct, provided it succeeds in checking the actual expansion directed toward the Asian frontiers of the Empire and does not at the same time result in creating in the Orient an Asiatic military power superior to those European nations whose advance it was deemed necessary to check.

The defeat of Russia by Japan resulted in four disastrous conditions:[1]

1. Instead of driving Russian expansion back upon Europe, it has diverted that power's advance from northeastern Asia to central Asia, where the most vital interests of the Empire are exposed upon frontiers which, if broken, will result in Imperial dissolution.

2. Japan has become more powerful in the Pacific than the British Empire.

3. Russian defeat resulted in the creation of the Japanese sphere of political and economic expansion that is inclusive of all British interests in the Pacific.

4. Russian defeat resulted in depriving England of her advantageous position of being the only insular power in the world by the creation of a second naval nation whose geographical relationship to Asia is identical with that of England to Europe, and its potentialities in the Pacific immeasurably greater than England's in the Atlantic.

By these four results of the Russo-Japanese War are betrayed the errors of British statesmanship and the wisdom of the Japanese.

In the Anglo-Japanese Alliance Japan conformed to those three principles laid down as determinate conditions in the formation of such compacts, while Great Britain overlooked essential factors that concerned the future interests of the Empire. It was in the renewal of this alliance that the Empire

[1] Chart III.

finally failed in its duty toward its Pacific dominions to even a greater degree than has Australasia failed in its subordination to Imperial interests and unity.

However essential it was that Russian advance in north China should be checked, the British Empire should have reserved to itself such freedom of action and balance of power that neither nation, in its victory, could secure that strategic position or military potentiality that would encroach upon or invade Saxon interests or act as a check upon their expansion.

In these principles, that should control the motives and formation of international alliances, the basic element is that no nation should assist in the creation or upbuilding or protection of any other state whose interests or lines of expansion are acutely convergent. Such aid only increases the capacity to expand, and augments their rate of movement along those given lines.

In the rise of Japan a new era has been ushered into the world. The predatory march of the West hesitates much in the same manner as that of the East some centuries ago. In this hesitation the British Empire is confronted with this condition: A second insular power has been born to live as it has lived, and to loot as it has looted the highways of the sea.

How significant is this fact was not realized at the time of its advent. Nor were the means employed to bring it about understood. It is only now dimly realized.

The destiny of Japan belongs to the future.

Japan is stronger in the Pacific than the British Empire is in the Atlantic.

Japan's naval control over the Pacific, comprising one-third of the world, is increasing in its absolute character, while the naval tenure of the Atlantic is becoming more and more tentative. Japan's military forces and their oceanic mobility are hardly inferior to the armies of Germany, while the expeditionary forces of the Empire are less than seven Japanese divisions.

Nations in their development are constrained to given lines by their geographical environment. Two nations situated in different parts of the world and inhabited by different races will progress along identical lines if the geography and climatic conditions of their respective countries are relatively the same. When, moreover, we find two nations whose welfare and greatness are dependent upon the acquisition of the same sources of wealth or power, and to secure which the same means are employed, then we are at once cognizant of this salient and at the same time ominous condition, that so long as these two nations continue to be of relative strength their interests and lines of expansion are so acutely convergent that in due time they enter into that fatal Punic era wherein even peace is war.

The Anglo-Japanese Alliance has made possible, in the fullest sense of the term, the Japanese Empire. It may result in giving over to her sovereignty one-third of the world. On the other hand, the British Empire not only has received no return from this arrangement, but has, on the contrary, been placed where the works of yesterday are the mines of to-day.

It is evident that whenever assistance is given another nation to curtail or destroy the political and territorial expansion of a common enemy it involves two obligations, neither of which in this instance was observed. So that by the time this alliance comes to an end we will find the Indian frontiers more vulnerable than ever — the western marches of China occupied, and Japan impregnable in the Pacific.

The forces that constitute the propulsion of Japanese expansion are apparent; but the direction that it will take has still the appearance of being wrapped in mystery. It should, however, be manifest as the forces themselves, since the expansion of nations is not an erratic progress, but is controlled and directed by known laws.

Japan's relation to Asia and the Pacific is identical with England's relation to Europe and the Atlantic prior to her Pacific expansion. The only difference between the extension of the Japanese Empire and that of England is that Japan's activities will be restricted to the Pacific, of which she constitutes the strategic center.[1] Japan's present continental extension of her empire is within her true

---

[1] *The Valor of Ignorance.*

scheme of expansion, as were England's continental wars a part of her development. Should Japan, to extend her sovereignty on the Asian continent, neglect to first gain control of the Pacific, then the duration of her national greatness will draw to an end.

The basic principle governing the growth and defense of an insular power not only belongs to the naval supremacy of the sea in which the nation is located, but, in modern times, the radii of this control must be lengthened in distance proportionately as the time to traverse them is shortened by the increasing rapidity and capacity of modern transportation. Because of this law Japan's maritime frontiers must extend eastward of the Hawaiian Islands and southward of the Philippines. For Japan not to possess the control of the Pacific is to lose her sovereignty in Asia, and would be equivalent to England warring against Germany with the latter in control of the Atlantic. Because of this Japan draws near to her next war—a war with America—by which she expects to lay the true foundation of her greatness.[1]

The Republic's indifference to the development and potentiality of Japan, its submersion in the ebb and flux of party politics, its heterogeneous racial elements, the supremacy of the individual over the welfare of the nation, and, finally, the nation's vain and tragic scorn of the soldier, predetermines the consummation of this fatal combat.

[1] *The Valor of Ignorance.*

Subsequent to this war the strategic position of the British Empire in the Pacific becomes so vulnerable as to be subject to the will of Japan.[1] And as in the same manner Wei-Hai-Wei is now rendered useless by Port Arthur, Korea, and the Japanese Islands, so will Hongkong be wedged in between Formosa and the Philippines, Singapore segregated, and Australasia cut off from North America.

Should the British Empire, following this war and the expiration of the alliance, become involved in Europe or on the Indian frontiers, her defeat would result in the eventual inclusion of Australasia under Japanese sovereignty. Japan will not falter nor hesitate to give expression to that basic principle already laid down, that there must be no cessation to the militant growth and expansion of a nation if it is to survive.

When we consider what constitutes the essentials of national power and supremacy over other nations, realizing at the same time that they are all-potential in Japan, we may well halt and wonder. While the militancy of our race has been decreasing proportionately with the increased complexity of our civilization, there exists no such deterioration in Japan; for what we evolved slowly with the wear and tear of it upon our militancy they have taken as a whole, and strapped, or perhaps, as time will determine, welded, it to their valor.

In the re-establishment of the political and mili-

---

[1] *The Valor of Ignorance.*

tary equilibrium of the Pacific the British Empire has not only to consider the strategic impregnability of Japan's position, but Japan itself and the character of the elements that constitute it. Here the vain and ignorant populace has no place in the conduct of the affairs of the nation, and the loud noises of haranguing multitudes carry no intimidation into the council-chambers of the state. Silently, without haste, slowly, with an intentness which is conscious of neither hesitation nor diversion, this militant empire moves across the sea. The nation vanishes. It has been metamorphosed into a soldier. This soldier is the genius of the nation. He has elevated martyrdom to heroism, and heroism to duty. He does not haggle over eternity, but, having found a God in his country, has discovered a sanctuary in his valor.

The restoration of the former equilibrium in the Pacific, where a balance of power will make all conquest tentative and prevent the tenure of this third of the world from passing under the sovereignty of an alien power, is a duty that the Empire not only owes to its Pacific dominions, but to itself, of which they constitute a component part. Their isolation presages the eventual shrinkage and dissolution of the same inevitability as would the loss of a more vital portion of the Empire entail. Time alone is the differentiating principle.

The permanent defense of Australasia in the future is not only naval, but belongs to a navy whose

combative strength is equal to or exceeds that of
the strongest naval power in the Pacific. This, it
is evident, can only be accomplished by the Empire
in its entirety.

The political and military equilibrium of the
Pacific is not, primarily, opposition to Japan. It
belongs to a relative equalization of power among
Pacific nations, so that the British Empire is able
to maintain, in its capacity of a Pacific state, that
balance of power which will insure the integrity
of its possessions and interests.

From those principles already considered as determining the potential character of alliance, and the
policy of supporting an Oriental nation against the
Asiatic expansion of a European power, it is evident that China, and not Japan, was the nation with
whom such an alliance should have been made.
While this was impossible at the time the agreement
was entered into, on account of the weakness of
that nation, it should have been the policy of the
British Empire years before such an alliance was
necessary to create in China a great continental
power. This necessity still remains and is reducible
to three conditions.

The frontiers of China are contiguous with those
of Russia from the Pamir to the Pacific for a distance of over six thousand miles, and form, with
the Indian boundaries, homogeneous frontiers having such interests in common against the aggression of Russia that their allegiance is perma-

nent, and not the temporary expedient of statesmen.

China is even more than Russia a continental nation. Its development, its policy, and military expansion will be controlled by those characteristics which govern the development of such a state. The expansion of China is antagonistic to Russia more than to any other nation. Had Russia attempted the strengthening of China, as the British Empire succeeded in doing for Japan, Russia would have committed the same mistake. As British and Japanese progression are basically convergent on the sea, so are Russia and China convergent on land. It is this convergence that constitutes the value of China's alliance to the Empire. With the development of China and a diffusion of its central population along the railroads which will be constructed to its northern and western frontiers, it can be said that the worth of this alliance increases proportionately with China's increase in power and extension of her empire. This is the reverse of Saxon relations with Japan.

The principle of protecting India from Russia through the continuance of the Anglo-Japanese Alliance is one of those tragic delusions which are, from time to time, forced upon nations. To understand that Russian victory would affect the security of India was not difficult; but to realize that Russian defeat increased the vulnerability of these frontiers to even a greater extent did not occur to the British nation. In this bitter paradox we find, moreover, that the destruction of British power in India results not alone in Russian supremacy on the Asian continent, but eliminates Saxon power from the Pacific and extends Japanese maritime sovereignty over the whole of it. Japan and Russia are natural allies — not Japan and England. The true extension of their respective empires is not convergent. One is continental, the other maritime. But more than that the Saxon race, which opposes Russian expansion by land, must in due time oppose with equal determination Japanese expansion by sea. A victory by either of these nations over the British Empire is equally fortuitous. The Saxon bars the natural expansion of both. This creates between them that cohesive community of interests, the destruction of the common enemy, that some day will result in a specific alliance.

China presents the opposite of the above conditions. While Japan could consummate her ambitions for Pacific supremacy through the conquest of India by Russia, such a conquest would for China presage her eventual destruction. The interest of China in the preservation of India's integrity is as essential to her as the security of her own territorial and political entity. Russian conquest of China determines, to an equal degree, the eventual destruction of British power in India. So identical are the interests of China and the British Empire that, while their progression and expansion affect a common enemy, the expansion or greatness of that enemy or its allies is as invariably dangerous to one as the other. Danger, therefore, consolidates the interests of these two empires, and prosperity does not draw them apart.

It is not alone the interdependence of China and the British Empire for the preservation of their political and territorial integrity in Asia that determines the natural character of their relationship; but the same fact is true in every phase of their national activities and expansion. The same characteristics that make Russia and Japan allies belong also to China and the British Empire. While Russian expansion is continental, so also is China's; while Japan's expansion is maritime, so is that of the Saxons. There is no national convergence of interests, and where this does not exist that antagonism which results in war cannot arise. What the Saxon sea power is to China, China's land forces are to the Empire—a defense that neither nation can alone evolve. The extension of these militant activities being entirely counterbalanced can never hold for the other those future dangers which are the product of an alliance with a nation whose expansion is convergent.

An alliance with a rehabilitated China results in the restoration of the political and military equilibrium not only in the western Pacific, but to an almost equal degree in Central Asia. On the other hand, China, continued in chronic decadence, increases proportionately the dangers which threaten Saxon dominion in Asia and the Pacific. While the conquest of India predetermines the fate of China, so with equal certitude can we say that the dissolution of China only precedes the expulsion of Saxon power from Asia and the western Pacific.

VIII

THE SAXON AND THE RUSSIAN

Self-segregation of the East Now Impossible.—Convergence of European Interests in Asia.—Predetermined Expansion of Russia.—Three Homogeneous Lines of.—India's Importance to.

AS we study the evolution and development of the human race relative to the political intercourse of its parts, we are confronted for the first time in its history with this singular condition: the association of Oriental nations with those of the Occident on a basis of equality and permanency in all the activities of political life. Heretofore the contact of the West with the East has been a clash, a struggle, then a recoil, each upon itself—except where one or the other remained hesitantly supreme over its spoil, or momentarily paramount amidst the debris of conquest.

Conditions permitting the voluntary self-segregation of the East and the West now no longer exist. Nations cannot in this age still hide themselves behind their mountain walls or their moats of space and sea. Their wealth or their poverty, their strength or their weakness, is known, not to a portion, but to the entire world. Science, unlike God, has no chosen people. Those by the sunrise and those by its going down are one and the same. It has, in its impartial and relentless manner, crushed this once vast world into a little ball around which go, each day, the whisperings of a hundred tongues. It is now a hundred cubits less in size than the Tower of Babel. So small has this once immeasurable world become that man sees all its sides at once. He hears simultaneously all its noises. He knows each day the storm and sunshine of every quarter; the quarrels and laughter, the hunger and waste, the hates and deception still toiling on in these old and new lands where, simultaneously, man boycots time and God and space.

But what does this permanency, this equality, this crushed-together interassociation of the Orient with the Occident hold for the latter in its numerical inequality? Who is to say that it is not the renascence in a new and terrible earnestness of the old menace?

Mankind, both as individuals and as nations, is moved, in all his essential activities, by motives that have their origin in defined primal instincts. The antagonism of the East to the West, and conversely, belongs wholly to this basic principle: the struggle for survival and mastery between the two predominant races of mankind.

While it is true that changed association, altered environment, and numerous other mutual conditions have a corresponding effect upon and modification of prior racial characteristics, yet this alteration is not instantaneous, but extends over a period of time relatively long or short, as determined by the character of the change, whether it belongs to custom, to racial characteristics, or to primitive human instincts. Man constantly deceives himself by believing in the rapidity of such transformation by failing to differentiate between these three conditions.

Because the customs of the Orient have changed, that they have adopted the essentials of Occidental civilization, does not mean a concurrent change in their racial peculiarities or tendencies nor a simultaneous metamorphosis of more primal attributes which complete the distinction between them and the Occidental. Such changes as these can only take place after long periods of time as compared to the adoption and even assimilation of customs and outward forms of another race.

Who, then, would assert that the old antagonism of the East and West has vanished because distance between them has been reduced? To decrease distance between antagonisms is to increase proportionately their intensity. To augment the probabilities of a struggle it is only necessary to increase the proximity of antagonists. Though the means of warfare and the manner of its conduct are no longer those by which Alexander waded his way to the Orient, or by which Genghis Khan fell upon Europe, yet the causation of this everlasting struggle remains the same.

Mukden is only an echo of Arbela.

The sudden crowding together of the East and the West through the medium of science does not mean, therefore, the cessation or elimination of their combats and contentions. It only signifies that their warfare, which was at one time as intermittent as the tempests of Koko Nor, has now become a factor in the ebb and flow of their affairs that is constant in causation and effect. It is the immutable character of this confused struggle that necessitates a political readjustment of the entire world and postpones to a dim and uncertain future the fulfilment of that despairing cry of "Peace on Earth."

We have witnessed in Europe from time to time those long periods of war that preceded and were concurrent with every readjustment of political conditions. This the progression of mankind necessitates at unequal intervals, not only in Europe, but in every portion of the globe where races of men live adjacent to one another in separate political entities. Though the wars of the seventeenth, eighteenth, and nineteenth centuries for the adjustment of European politics were believed to be, in their time, final, yet Europe even now prepares to enter upon the old combat. The Punic Wars have been forgotten, and the Napoleonic struggles have been stilled for a hundred years; yet the causes through all these centuries remain identical in their basic impulse, unaltered except in the manner of their expression.

When, however, we consider the world, instead of Europe, and all its diverse races, encompassed in a combative area less than that continent, we may realize, though ever so dimly, the portent of this dreadful fact: that we are just entering upon the first era of this political readjustment of the world; that these eras will succeed one another with the same inevitability as do the recurring cycles of Time.

How pitiful it is, in the realization of these facts, to behold a great race padding itself with the valor of its forefathers and, at the same time, shirking those struggles upon which depends their racial greatness and survival. No line of demarcation between cowardice and evasion exists, whether it is individual or national. To attempt to escape responsibility by subterfuge is only the consummation of fear.

For the survivors of those who crucify their race under the delusion that they can deride the God that led it, there remains only an endless, country-less trek forever.

The political readjustment of the world, due to the circumstances we have mentioned, does not alone concern contentions between the white and colored races; but, on the other hand, the approaching period of adjustment will be more or less restricted on the Asian continent to those white races whose expansion and interests in Asia have been and are convergent. This acuteness in the convergence of European interests in Asia has resulted from two conditions:

1. The reduction of communicable time and distance by mechanical invention.

2. The awakening of Asia.

In direct ratio to the increase of effectiveness in these two conditions has the convergence of European interests in Asia been increased and the rate of their expansion augmented in intensity. Of the nations most affected by these altered circumstances France is least concerned, and the British Empire most, since the Asiatic convergences of both Germany and Russia are directed against the strategic center of British Asia.

We have heretofore called attention to a strange fatality that, from time to time, seizes hold upon all nations, and in numerous instances is the indirect cause that leads to their final dissolution. This characteristic is concentrating the entire attention of the nation against one enemy, while the movement against its other frontiers by an equally dangerous foe remains unchecked. This has never been more completely exemplified than by the British nation. In its fear of German conquest it has concealed from itself the advance of Russia against that portion of the Empire which, if once seized, destroys it more effectually than the German invasion of England.

In the development of the Russian Empire man has more nearly approached those characteristics

that mark the measured, unhurried growth of
Nature. In its extension it has moved onward
with elemental propulsion. Like a glacier, its movement is only apparent by periods of time. So imperceptible is the terrible, imperturbable grind of its
way that we do not perceive its progress until it
has passed a given point. What it does not crush
it erodes. What it does not erode it forces on in
front until into some crevasse, great or small, it
pushes the debris that impedes its way.

It moves on.

It was this glacial, timeless, measured movement,
this calm and dreadful certitude, that even terri-
fied Napoleon when the breath of it chilled into
cinders his highway of flame.

At the beginning of the eighteenth century Russia was less than two hundred and seventy-five
thousand square miles. In seven generations it increased until it comprised nearly nine millions, or
one-seventh of the land surface of the world. Russia in Europe alone is now larger than all other
European nations. During the same period of
time its population increased from twelve millions
to more than one hundred and fifty millions. At
its present rate of increase, by propagation alone,
it will exceed four hundred millions in three generations. From the beginning of the eighteenth
century to the present time there has been a corresponding increase in its revenue from one million
pounds to more than two hundred million.

It is, however, not this net result of Russian growth and greatness that inspires us with those feelings of its invincibility to which we have just given expression, but rather the manner of this progression. The expansion of Russia, unlike that of most great empires, has never been erratic nor dependable upon fortuitous circumstances. Instead of being the result of an aggregate of fortunate expedients, it has been the ruthless exemplification of a predetermined plan.

At the beginning of the eighteenth century Russia was consolidated to the extent that it was possible to proceed definitely to that expansion decided upon during the seventeenth century. In the preceding hundred years five lines of expansion had been predetermined:[1]

1. In the northwest to force Sweden from the Baltic littoral and establish the Russian frontier on that sea. This work had been begun by the Tsars John III. and IV.

2. In the west to gain Little and White Russia from Poland. This work had been begun by the Tsar Alexei-Michaelovitch.

3. In the south to gain the Black Sea, to create unrest in Turkey preparatory to invasion. This work had been laid out by the Grand Dukes Oleg and Sviatosloff.

4. In the southeast to secure the Caspian Sea and the Caucasus. This work had been begun by

[1] Kuropatkin.

the Tsars Theodore - Ivanovitch and Boris Godunoff.

5. In the east to move toward the Pacific and
India.

During the eighteenth century, for which these
five labors had been predetermined, only three were
accomplished. On the northwest frontier, constituting at that time the most essential line of
Russian expansion, the control of the Baltic, Russia,
after twenty-one years of war, completed this work,
and in the destruction of Swedish power assumed
that supremacy in the north that has never yet
been altered. On the western frontier, to gain
Little and White Russia, necessitated three wars
with Poland. These struggles ended not only in
the consolidation of these portions of Russia with the
empire, but in the destruction of Poland as an independent kingdom. The advance toward the
Black Sea and the weakening of Turkey resulted
in four wars with that power, the first ending in
Russian defeat, as did the initial campaign against
Sweden; but in the fourth the object of Russian
advance was accomplished. Russia had reached
the Black Sea, possessed the Crimea and the lands
beyond the Dniester and the Bug.

The nineteenth century was only a continuation
of Russian expansion and consolidation. On the
northwest frontiers, after a war of fifteen months,
Finland was annexed to the empire. On the west
Poland was dismembered and a portion added to

Russia. The extension of Russian sovereignty and its consolidation on the Black Sea resulted in three more wars with Turkey and one with a European coalition. The first ended with the annexation of a part of Bessarabia; the second in securing the mouths of the Danube and three hundred and seventy miles of the Black Sea littoral; the third in the acquisition of Batoum and Kars.

During the eighteenth century no movement had been made on the eastern line of expansion; and an effort in the direction of India had ended during the early part of the eighteenth century in the repulse at Khiva. This apparent restriction of Russian activities to the expansion of its European frontiers during the whole of the eighteenth century led Europe to believe that the extension of Russia to the Pacific and the conquest of India had been put aside forever. Yet, during this time, the predestined movement of Russia toward the Pacific and India was going on, without noise or bluster, imperceptibly and glacier-like. Its progress was only noted when it passed a given point.

In the nineteenth century, to gain dominion over the Caucasus and the Caspian, Russia fought two wars with Persia and a war of sixty-two years with the highlanders of the Caucasus. In Central Asia wars were carried on for thirty years to gain the Afghan frontiers of India. During this same century Russia gained the Pacific by the annexation of Amur and Ussure regions, Kamchatka, and the peninsula of Kwang-tung. It consolidated and drew together in one compact mass the whole of these vast possessions.

Russia is European. It is also Asian.

As we follow the expansion and study the development of this nation from those plans determined upon in the seventeenth century, we seem to contemplate the gradual evolution of some irrepressible natural force rather than the struggle of man. During these two centuries twenty-one wars were fought for the expansion of the empire lasting for one hundred and one years.[1] To secure the Baltic it was necessary to sacrifice 700,000 men of 1,800,000 put into the field; to gain the Black Sea 750,000 perished out of 3,200,000.

Russia in her progress is concerned no more with the devastation of her wars than is Russian nature with the havoc of her winters. In the eighteenth century this empire sent into her wars 4,910,000 troops; casualties of which were 1,380,000. In the nineteenth century the number of troops engaged was 4,900,000; the casualties, 1,410,000. Yet the population of Russia at the beginning of the eighteenth century was only twelve million; at the beginning of the nineteenth only thirty-eight million. When, therefore, in consideration of these facts, we contemplate the possibilities of Russian expansion during the twentieth century,[2] we are conscious of a potential power for aggression which, relative to

[1] Kuropatkin.   [2] Chart III.

the forces that must be overcome, is far greater than during the eighteenth and the nineteenth centuries.

As we regard those plans made in the seventeenth century for the expansion of the Russian Empire, and have for two hundred years witnessed the fortitude and determination with which they have been pursued, we are unable to believe in their voluntary abandonment. Heretofore, these same Russians have never faltered, never hesitated; without haste, always hopeful in defeat, reticent in victory, never seeing the ground they have furrowed with combat and hillocked with their dead; keeping their eyes constantly on those distant yet defined horizons toward which they have been directed. The beginning of the eighteenth century found Russia moving toward those objectives. From that time until the present they have not been led into new ambitions, nor have they ever lost sight of those racial goals determined upon by their ancestors. While, of the five tasks laid down for the work of the eighteenth century, only three were actively engaged in, the other two were put aside for the work of the succeeding century. In the same manner the empire of the nineteenth century postponed to the twentieth the consummation of these works.

The twentieth century opened with the defeat of the empire in Manchuria, involving Russia in serious circumstances. Defeat is an old tragedy with Russia. It marks for her the beginning of a new century. The eighteenth began at Narva; the nineteenth with Austerlitz; the twentieth with Mukden. But Narva was followed by Poltava, though twenty-one years elapsed before the Swedish power was broken. Austerlitz and Friedland were followed by Moscow and the seizure of Paris. Who shall say that there is not a sequel to Mukden?

Russian aggression in Europe during the eighteenth century made possible the expansion of the succeeding period, and from this, in turn, the expansion of the twentieth century receives its impulse.[1] At the beginning of this century there existed three homogeneous lines of Russian expansion:

1. On the right flank to the Bosphorus.
2. On the left flank to and along the Pacific.
3. On the center to India through Persia.

It is in the study of these three lines of expansion that we realize the significance of the rise of Japan and its victory, the rise of Germany and its ambitions, as they affect the Saxon and Russian in forcing these two powers with increasing intensity into that war settled upon so many generations ago.

Nations, much in the same manner as individuals, either move along lines of least resistance or undertake those labors by which the greatest returns are to be secured from the energy expended. When, however, there is given to nations, as to individuals, the choice of two or more lines along which they must progress, and since one of the lines is pre-eminent in

[1] Chart III.

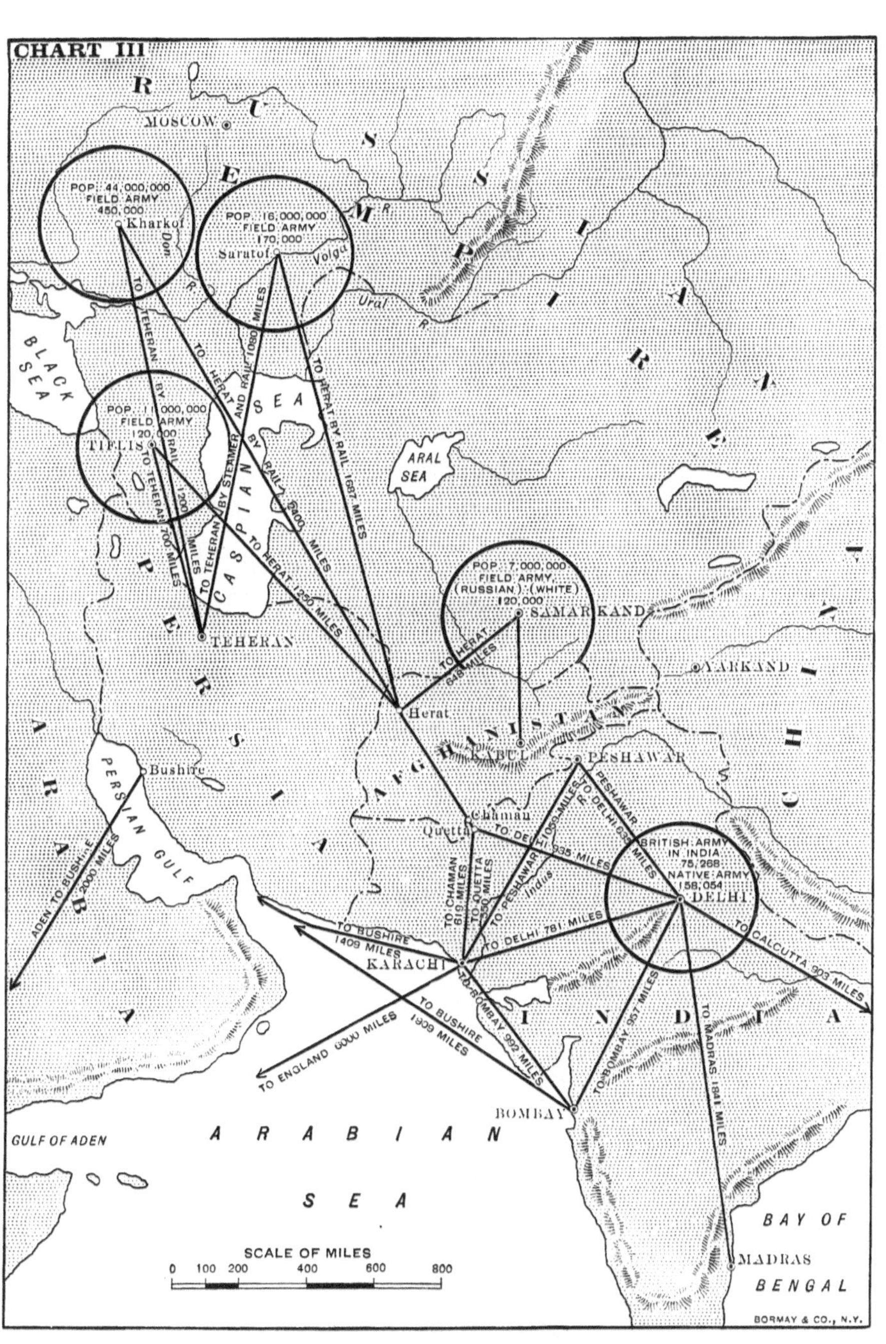

CHART III
MOSCOW
POP. 44,000,000 FIELD ARMY 450,000
Kharkof
Don
POP. 16,000,000 FIELD ARMY 170,000
Saratof
Volga
Ural
BLACK SEA
POP. 11,000,000 FIELD ARMY 120,000
TIFLIS
CASPIAN SEA
TO TEHERAN BY RAIL, 1080 MILES
TO HERAT BY STEAMER AND RAIL, 2000 MILES
BY RAIL, 2000 MILES
TO HERAT BY RAIL, 1687 MILES
TO TEHERAN, 600 MILES
TO TEHERAN 700 MILES
TO HERAT 1200 MILES
ARAL SEA
POP. 7,000,000 FIELD ARMY (RUSSIAN) (WHITE) 120,000
SAMARKAND
YARKAND
TEHERAN
TO HERAT 648 MILES
Herat
KABUL
PESHAWAR
R. DELHI 683 MILES
AFGHANISTAN
TO DELHI 1095 MILES
PERSIAN GULF
Bushire
Chaman
Quetta
Indus
TO CHAMAN 619 MILES
TO QUETTA 536 MILES
TO PESHAWAR 935 MILES
TO DELHI 781 MILES
BRITISH ARMY IN INDIA 75,268 NATIVE ARMY 158,054
DELHI
TO CALCUTTA 903 MILES
ADEN TO BUSHIRE 2000 MILES
TO BUSHIRE 1409 MILES
KARACHI
TO BOMBAY 992 MILES
TO BOMBAY 957 MILES
TO MADRAS 1841 MILES
TO ENGLAND 6000 MILES
TO BUSHIRE 1909 MILES
INDIA
ARABIA
BOMBAY
GULF OF ADEN
ARABIAN
SEA
BAY OF
MADRAS
BENGAL
SCALE OF MILES
0 100 200 400 600 800
BORMAY & CO., N.Y.

its importance, the correct choice is seldom made, since it stands in inverse ratio to the number of lines to be chosen from. Hence, in regard to the time, the Russian expansion of its left flank to the Pacific was ten years later than it should have been. The advance of its right flank on Turkey, as regards time, should have been made immediately subsequent to the Treaty of Tilsit. The advance on India, as regards time, is the present, as we will hereafter show.

In a previous chapter has been shown that the strategic position of India is pre-eminent. As a part of Russia its importance would be so augmented that it becomes, in the possession of Russia, more nearly the key to universal empire than any other portion of the globe. Modern civilization, with its elimination of distance by its mechanical inventions, has brought suddenly upon the consciousness of the world this half-world dominion of the Indian sphere; yet it has been co-existent from remotest antiquity.

While England gained control of this vast region through the valor of her soldiers, the Saxon people have not up to the present become cognizant of the fact that it is upon India that their Empire rests. On the other hand, while Russian soldiers have still to march for the first time upon Indian soil, yet its conquest has always formed the basic principle of Russian expansion. When in that old, eventful hour the five corner-stones of the Russian nation were laid down, India was the one upon which the main edifice of the empire was to be placed. It is, therefore, a melancholy affair when we compare the self-blindness of our own race in this age with the prescience of that monarch Peter, who, more than two hundred years ago, wrote down for the guidance of his people these memorable words: ''Bear in mind that the commerce of India is the commerce of the world, and that he who can exclusively control it is the Master of Europe; no occasion should, therefore, be lost to provoke war with Persia, to hasten its decay, and to advance to the Persian Gulf.''

When there exists several lines of national expansion, the choice of and adherence to the basic line is one of the most difficult tasks in the progression of national life. It seldom if ever finds constant expression, but varies in accordance with the shifting of national politics—either as they are altered by the wisdom or ignorance of successive reigns, or by those exterior causes inherent in the growth or decay of adjacent states. While the principle of Russian occupation of India remains as immutable to-day as during the age of Peter the Great, the effect of such a conquest upon the entire world is immeasurably more decisive than during his time.

When the Tsar Alexander, immediately subsequent to the signing of the Treaty of Tilsit, did not force the extension of Russia to the Bosphorus by way of the Balkans, the opportunity passed away. No longer can the empire progress directly along its right flank; and with each successive decade the impossibility of returning to it is augmented. Each new increment to German power decreases proportionately Russia's capacity to return again to this direct expansion through the Balkans. But this does not prohibit Russian progress to the Bosphorus. It has only diverted her, lengthened her way, and altered the manner of its accomplishment.

We have shown [1] that the strategic sphere of India on the west is inclusive of the strategic triangle—India, Teheran, and Port Said—within which is Mesopotamia, the Tigris, and the Euphrates. With the occupation of Persia and India all that which is now Saxon becomes Russian; and Asia Minor, in due time, will pass under her dominion. Russia then approaches the Bosphorus by the southern bank. So long as German military power and Austrian military power remain constant in their positive progression, and the Saxon defense of India and its sphere remains constant in its deterioration, then the line of least resistance for Russian advance to the Bosphorus is by way of Persia and India. Whenever the Russian armies look out over the Indian Ocean they can cry out truthfully, "We have reached the Bosphorus!"

When Russia began, in the latter part of the nine-

[1] Chart I.

teenth century, the expansion of her left flank through Siberia to the Pacific, it was correct in principle.   With the completion of the Siberian railway that seaboard ceased to be distant from the heart of the empire.   It became possible to reach the Pacific from Moscow in less time than it required, at the beginning of the same century, to travel to St. Petersburg.   But so subordinate is this line of imperial extension to that upon India that it should have only necessitated a corresponding degree of military exertion.   That the results to be gained from the expenditure required on this left flank can never be commensurate is due to four facts:

1. Had a war with Japan occurred prior to or immediately subsequent to the Chinese-Japanese War, only then would the degree of expenditure have been small enough to be commensurate with the benefits derived from reaching the Pacific seaboard.   This is determinable by comparing the inability of such force to accomplish like results in an advance against Persia and India.

2. The benefits accruing to Russia subsequent to Russian victory in the war of 1904 would not have been commensurate with the cost Russia did incur. This is determinable by comparing the results obtainable from an identic effort against Persia and India.

3. That in the future any Russian advance against the north Pacific will entail a minimum of expendi-

ture that will be in excess of the maximum expenditure of the war of 1904–05.

4. Each new increment to Japanese power decreases proportionately Russian capacity to move along this line.

Such is the result of Japan's victory. Russia has, in her advance to the Pacific, been cast back much in the same manner as she was turned aside from her old highway through the Balkans. But these repulses, strange as it may seem, accelerate rather than retard Russian expansion. So exact has this result been that we can reduce it to this almost invariable law: that the impulse of Russian expansion along alternate lines is measured by the degree of retrocession on other lines of aggression, the ratio of expansion to that of retrogression being as three is to two. It is because of this law that Russia continues to spread over Asia and Europe in defeat as well as in victory.

For the Russian the Japanese War was only a repulse. For the Saxon race it was a disaster. When Japan forced Russia back from the north Pacific, it was upon India that she hurled this great empire.

We have already shown that the strategic sphere of India in the East is inclusive of the triangle [1]— India, Hongkong, Singapore. The conquest of India would then insure her, in the possession of this strategic triangle, the control of those Far

[1] Chart I.

Eastern regions which are now under Saxon dominion.   By this Russia would segregate by land and by
sea the whole of the Orient from the whole of Europe.
Hurled back from the Pacific by Japan, and from
the Bosphorus by Germany, Russia is now forced
to her basic line of expansion, through Persia to the
Plains of India, where are found both the Pacific
and the Bosphorus.

IX

THE SAXON AND EUROPE

Russian Expansion Concentrated by Disaster.—Conditions Governing Alliances Made against a Common Objective.—Coalition
Directed against England.—Causes of Its Formation.—Results
to Each Nation.—Danger of German Expansion.

TO Russia, having learned the philosophy of
disaster, there comes no final defeat. Her
policy of predetermined expansion, while cumulative
with victory, is, on the other hand, concentrated by
disaster. This concentration of national forces
through national misfortune insures the empire
not only against destruction from external forces,
but eventual victory. Holding the interior lines of
Eurasia, her radii of aggression are directed against
those diverse portions of the world that are politically and geographically incapable of cohesive
coalition. When Russian movement is checked in
one sphere the propulsion of her expansion in other
spheres receives that proportionate impetus we have
indicated. The expansion of Russia in its intensity
never ceases. Those tides that recede from one
shore recede only to break upon another. Oceanic
in its greatness, it is oceanic in the expression of its
forces.

The cumulative effect of Russian victory in the extension of the empire is shown by the expansion of her center line, the conquest of White Russia being succeeded by that of Little and Southern Russia; these by the conquest of the Black Sea, the Caucasus, and central Asia. This center will in due time move on to that natural objective determined upon two centuries ago. The conquest of Persia will be followed by that of India, by the control of Asia Minor and its environment on the west, Burma and its environment on the east.[1] The possession of the Red Sea and the Indian Ocean will then give to Russia the same domination in Africa and the Pacific now held by the Saxon race.

At this period the Russian Empire draws to a close.

It approaches the Empire of the World.

The concentration of Russian propulsion through disaster is not an anomalous condition, but is a natural sequence due to three factors:

1. The territorial homogeneity and interior strategic situation of Russia relative to Asia and Europe.

2. The geographical, racial, and political segregation of the nations constituting Russian frontiers.

3. The automatic adjustment of Russian military equilibrium as regulated by the maximum military expansion of her strongest neighbor.

The beginning of the eighteenth century opened with the defeat of Russia at Narva. The propul-

[1] Chart II.

sion and concentration given to Russian expansion
by this disaster resulted in an increase of power
which exceeded that of Sweden, her strongest neighbor, and led to the expansion of Russia south and
eastward. On the other hand, the nineteenth century began with Russian defeat at Austerlitz, and
resulted in that military development which brought
about the expansion of the empire south and eastward during the nineteenth century. These two
elemental defeats increased indirectly the Russian
Empire from less than three hundred thousand
square miles to more than nine million. The twentieth century, like the two previous, opened with the
third elemental defeat of Russia by Japan. The
result of this war will be the same as disasters in
the past; the same concentration and the same increase in the propulsion of Russian expansion in
other spheres when the old augmentation and rehabilitation of these forces have been accomplished.
Had Germany, instead of Japan, been responsible
for this defeat of Russia at the commencement of
the twentieth century, the result would have been the
same, except (1) that the degree of Russia's military
rehabilitation would have been as much greater as
Germany is militarily stronger than Japan, and as
the interests involved are more vital; (2) that the
sphere of subsequent Russian expansion might have
been in northwest Asia instead of Persia and India.

During this century Russian aggression, subsequent to the readjustment of her military power,

seeks that line of expansion where the minimum of resistance is to be found commensurate with the means employed and the results gained. This we have already shown is in central Asia, Persia, and India, since the Saxon defenses of these regions have, relative to Russia's increased opportunities and capacity, fallen so low as to be almost a negligible quantity, while the gains of victory to Russia have increased in inverse ratio. On the other hand, the defenses of the Balkans by the Teutons and northeast Asia by the Japanese have been augmented to such a degree that the rewards of success would not, in the beginning of this century, be commensurate to the labor and expenditure required of the Russian Empire. The result of this is the concentration of Russian expansion to central Asia, Persia, and India.

This résumé now brings us to the consideration of that fatal interpolitical relationship of Russia, Japan, and Germany, which has now assumed through the agency of natural forces a coalition directed against the survival of Saxon supremacy. In this dreadful *Dreibund* statesmen have played but little part. It is the result of a succession of fatalities which, delimiting the control of man, resolves it back to those basic principles we have shown to be immutable. They vary only in the manner in which they affect the duration of national existence or its circumscription.

Alliances made by man and directed against a

common objective conform to two conditions: they are made for mutual self-protection or mutual gain. Strange as it may appear, those coalitions made for common gain are stronger than those made for mutual safety. The reason for this is simple. When a union is the result of mutual desire for gain, it is positive in its action; when the alliance is for mutual defense, the resultant action is negative. The coalition for gain is convergent, since it is the direction of different parts to a common objective. The coalition of defense is, on the other hand, divergent, since its movement is a retrocession from a common point to as many separate parts as there are members of the alliance.

When, however, we understand the significance of a coalition of races formed and directed by natural forces against a solitary and scattered race, we become cognizant of those eventualities that, in the near future, await the Saxon race. The *Dreibund* of Germany, Italy, and Austria is to the British Empire a negative menace. Being made by man and based on political considerations, it is as transient as it is artificial. Notwithstanding the effort of a member of the coalition to change the character of this alliance to one of aggression against the Saxon race, it will not occur. For the Teutons to succeed in reversing the *motif* of this coalition from one of defense to one of aggression, it must insure to Italy, subsequent to the dissolution of the British Empire, that degree of gain which would permit of her future national expansion being independent of the Teutonic. The reverse of this would happen. Germany, because of her vast initial power, and not Italy, would, subsequent to the overthrow of the British Empire, succeed to the control of the Mediterranean and all that which is now British in or upon its shores. Italy would then become no longer free to pursue even her present circumscribed destiny, but would pass completely under Teutonic domination not only by land, but by sea.

It can be considered as a maxim that in exact ratio as the Teutonic race increases in power and domination the Italian kingdom decreases proportionately in these two factors. Because it is paradoxical that Italian national security is inherent, not in the successes of its allies, but in their destruction, do we finally ascertain the fallacious and artificial character of this *Dreibund*, in so far as the future of Italy is concerned in the dissolution of the British Empire.

We now pass from this ephemeral coalition instituted by man to the consideration of that other *Dreibund* which is the product of natural forces and forms a definite segment in the curve of history by which, knowing the causes of its formation, we are able to determine its progression and consummation. In the constitution of a coalition directed against the British Empire there are only three nations—Japan, Russia, and Germany—that can become parties to such an agreement wherein their efforts and responsibilities, singly and in coalition, are not in disproportion to their gains. This is due to three factors:

1. The policies of these three nations will not be vitally convergent until after the dissolution of the British Empire, since the primary radii of their political and geographical expansion are directed against the dominions of the Saxon race.

2. That so long as ordinary political intelligence is exercised and the passions of their respective populace do not intervene, there will be no internal disruption of this natural coalition, since:

(*a*) A war between Russia and Germany, while resulting disastrously to the defeated nation, brings no gains to the victor that would be commensurate with the expenditures.

(*b*) A war between Japan and Germany would result negatively to both victor and vanquished, while Russia would receive no advantage, since the geographical location plus the approximation of the military progression of these two nations prevents a decisive blow and leaves both nations at the conclusion of the war militarily stronger than at its beginning.

(*c*) A second war between Russia and Japan would again result negatively to both nations, except such territorial increments acquired from China, which are not commensurate with the expenditure made by either nation. Germany would gain no advantage, but would, on the other hand, be loser in a general sense from the increased militancy of both nations. A Japanese victory would increase the insecurity of her tenure in east Asia and the Pacific. A Russian victory would decrease the rate and security of her propulsion in the Balkans.

3. The dismemberment or defeat of the British Empire, on the other hand, results advantageously alike to Germany, Japan, and Russia. The gain to these nations is measured by the degree of completeness of British ruin. The gain accruing to each of these empires from the destruction of the British Empire is manifold greater than the maximum expenditure required from any one of them, or all in coalition. Should the dissolution of Saxon power originate in the conquest of India by Russia, or through the supremacy of Japan in the Pacific, or by the invasion of the United Kingdom by Germany, the result is the same as if these activities were predetermined by the three nations and were simultaneous in their occurrence. To Japan would go the predominance of the Pacific Ocean and its islands; to Russia that of the southern Asian continent and the Indian Ocean; to Germany that of western and southern Europe, the Mediterranean, and the Atlantic.

Such is this coalition constituted by natural forces and directed by natural laws; such are the causes of its formation, the manner and motives of its progression, the rewards and greatness resulting from the attainment of its ends. It is the unity of purpose inherent in the international progression of these three powers that must always be considered before preparation for the defense of the Saxon Empire is restricted specifically to any one of them.

We have heretofore dealt with the political and military growth of Japan,[1] its expansion in eastern Asia, and those necessities that predetermine its struggles with the Saxon for the ultimate sovereignty of the Pacific. We have considered the expansion of Russia southward and the conditions which lead toward the conquest of Persia and India. That we have reserved for so late a chapter the consideration of the expansion of Germany and the ruthless elbowing of its way into the dominions of the Saxon is due not to its less, but its greater importance. It is not that the Teutonic angle of convergence against the British Empire is more acute than that of Japan or Russia that determines its dangers, but because German convergence is directed against a more vital part of the Empire than is that of Japan, while the rate of propulsion with which it moves along this convergent line is greater than that of Russia in its expansion toward India. By this it is apparent that Japan's aggression against the Empire, relative to that of Germany, is remote in exact proportion as the sphere of expansion is less vital than that of the Teutons. The

[1] *The Valor of Ignorance.*

danger of Russian aggression, relative to that of the Germans, is remote as regards time, in exact proportion as Russia's rate of movement toward India is less than that of Germany against the United Kingdom.

Unfortunately, the Saxon race, because of the supremacy of individual ideals over those belonging to the nation or race, have become ignorant of the effects of racial unity and national cohesion. Because of this the basic dangers of Teutonic expansion remain to them unknown, while that knowledge which they should ascertain they seek to evade.

The convergence of the Teutonic and Saxon races to that ultimate point of contact which is war does not belong to those ephemeral causes that now agitate the British mind and out of which are manufactured the sorriest and pettiest fabrics of political strife. The supplanting of the British Empire by that of Germany has nothing to do primarily with the passions or hopes or fears of man, but is the exemplification of laws which have governed, from the beginning of human association, the rise and decline of nations.

The melancholy error that now burdens the British nation is this ignorance of the basic character of their danger—the fear, and not the knowledge, of their fate.

X

THE SAXON AND THE GERMAN

Law of Political Environment.—Tendency to Expand Dominant in First Struggles of a Race.—German Expansion Determined by German Power.—Future Relationship between the Saxon and Teuton.—Value of Holland, Denmark, and Austria to Germany.

IN this chapter will be considered but three of the successive stages by which the Germans have progressed toward war with the British Empire, a conflict which is apparent to Saxon consciousness, yet at the same time denied by it in the old way men and nations conceal from themselves all that is bitter and tragic.

One of the principal causes responsible for much that is erroneous in our ideas of national existence is due to the indifference with which we form our conceptions of the forces that control the formation, progress, and dissolution of states—the subordination of the individual to natural laws, and the circumscription or propulsion of his efforts. Conditions determined upon by environment are ordinarily known, but it is seldom recognized that nations are subordinates to like ordinances from which they also have no appeal. Their environment determines for them, as well as for individuals, the manner and the way of their progress.

In the environment of an individual there are numerous conditions more vital than that of his political peace; but to a nation the political environment is of such importance that it determines the possibilities and duration of national greatness. This law of political environment we state as follows:

1. National expansion moves in direction of those arcs constituting the nation's political environment, where the power of resistance is least and the propulsion is equal to or greater than toward any other arc.

2. National retrogression proceeds from those arcs of the nation's political environment where the inward power of resistance is least and the outward pressure equal to or greater than toward any other arc.

From the most ancient times until the present we have witnessed the unvarying application of this law—the attempted evasion of its decrees, and the ever-recurring futility of such efforts.

Of the nations now considered great all have grown powerful through the agency of this law. American expansion has never succeeded against Canada, the strongest arc in its political environment, but has invariably proceeded against those arcs least capable of resistance—against scattered Indian tribes, Mexicans, Hawaiians, and Spaniards. It has passed from the Western to the Eastern Hemisphere.

Russian expansion has been similar to that of

America. It has gone toward those arcs of its environment least capable of resistance. Eastward and southeastward its political government has been extended, while westward against those arcs whose power of resistance has exceeded that of Russian propulsion the frontiers have remained almost stationary.

On the other hand, though English sovereignty has been extended throughout all portions of the globe, it yet remains west of the English Channel. The lands closest to it are freest from its power. This condition has not been decreed by British statesmen, nor by the will of the English people, but has been due to the law just expressed, whereby the expansion of the British Empire has proceeded not with, but even contrary to, the volition of that nation.

By the operation of this same law is German expansion given its basic impulse. Only the manner of its expression and the degree of its propulsion are left to the will of the German people. The fundamental error in the English conception of German expansion is the belief that it results from some transient plan, the conception of an individual finding a momentary response in the German people.

Conditions, and not individuals, determine national expansion. Individuals, and not conditions, determine the manner and degree of its propulsion. When conditions productive of expansion occur during the lifetime of an individual whose genius grasps their significance and whose position in the state permits him to make use of his discernment, then occur those tragic epochs in national life when out of the wreckage of one state another is created. Such was the combination between Peter and Russia, Napoleon and France, Bismarck and Germany. To this combination the genius of such men is its soul.

Ordinarily this soul is transient.

In Germany it is otherwise.

The spirit of Bismarck has departed only to diffuse itself into the genius of his race. While other nations must await the suitable adjustment of conditions to human genius, Germany waits only for opportunity.

The British Empire, in its relationship to German expansion and the consequent dissolution of the British dominion, has not to deal with the German people, but only with conditions that determine Germanic expansion. The German nation waits only as Bismarck waited for conditions to shape themselves. So imbued is this race with his ideals that it can do without his genius. It has become Bismarckian. His heavy spirit has settled upon it. It wears his scowl. It has adopted his brutality, as it has his greatness. It has taken his criterion of truth, which is Germanic; his indifference to justice, which is savage; and his conception of a state, which is sublime.

This nation has forgotten God in its exaltation of the Germanic race.

THE SAXON AND THE GERMAN

In the development of Germany and its consequent relationship with the world no attempt has been made to differentiate between its future and that of the British Empire, which stands across the way it is soon to take.

A nation reaches its highest degree of wealth subsequent to its era of conquest and coincident with the limitation of its greatest power. But a nation, ceasing to expand, retrogrades. In national existence, as in individual, there is no permanency.

External weakness is determined by the degree of its internal power.

In the first struggles of a race the tendency to expand is most dominant. The more severe the struggle the more intense does this characteristic become. But when expansion, and the militancy that has made it possible, ceases, then the nation approaches the end of its political existence. Germany, on the one hand, and England, on the other, occupy these two extremes. The British Empire is accepted by its people as the culmination of their expansion; Germany has not entered upon its era of conquest as predetermined as it was for the Saxon.

The development of Germanic power is not recent. It had its origin in the philosophy of an Italian, its amplification by the labors of Frederic, its renascence by the genius of Bismarck. What Germany has done heretofore has only been a preparation. This is not completed. As yet Germany has sought no conquest. Its wars have been only for racial consolidation. It has not, in the true sense of expansion, gone beyond its own frontiers, yet has become more powerful than the Saxon nations. While they are politically disunited and geographically segregated, Germany is a single mass. From struggle and conquest the Saxon race now seeks, as others have sought, to leave the battle-fields of the world and yet retain through evasion and subterfuge the treasure of a thousand looted cities. The Teuton, emerging from his struggles to survive, steps forth upon this same battle-field of the world at the zenith of his militancy, and at the same time not less in wealth, in population, nor in potential power. On the one hand we find a bewildered race led hither and thither through labyrinthine ways; on the other, a military power in which neither theories nor sophistry find a place, but where the intentness of its aims knows no discouragement, its progress no diversion of the terribleness of its energy nor fatigue. The movement of such a nation resembles that of fate in the certitude of its progression. The noise of its approach tallies the destiny of many states.

It is difficult for the Saxon to understand that German expansion is not circumscribed by the European continent, but is determined only by the limitations of Teutonic power. This is due to the fact that natural obstacles as oceans, great distances by land, or unfavorable climatic conditions no longer limit the conquest of nations. Prussian troops can now be moved to the ends of the strategic world in less time than a hundred years ago they could go from Berlin to Paris. Owing to this elimination of space and time, while the geographical, political, and racial segregation of the balance of nations remains constant, Germany could, subsequent to the destruction of the British Empire, control her portion of the world with no greater difficulty than did Napoleon at one time direct the affairs of Europe.

There is no recognition in the British Empire of the actual conditions in which originate the propulsion of German expansion. This understanding is lost in the personal character the Saxon gives to war. But in neither the hate nor greed nor insolence of the Teutonic race is to be found the impulse of its expansion. The hate of a nation can be no greater than the hate of a single individual.

Races in their greater movements, such as now confront the Teutonic, are affected in their basic impulses, which are remote from individual passions. Ordinarily this propulsion comes from necessity.

Necessity is a racial god.

From time immemorial this god has led the treks of races, has furrowed the seas for their passage, and has with pillars of fire marked the way to the lands destined for them. Bismarck and the factories of Germany have again called down this god.

That German expansion must of necessity result in a struggle with the Saxon race is not due to Bismarck, nor to these same smoking chimneys, but belongs to the Saxon and Saxon activity. German expansion is only brought in conflict with those nations whose territories and suzerainty barricade its progression. And in proportion as they block Teutonic power, to the same degree are German energies directed toward the destruction of that power. If the Saxon race were situated, relative to the lines of German expansion, as are the Spanish and Italian, the improbabilities of war would be in like proportion. While Spain and Italy are removed from the sphere of German growth, German political and geographical progression are encompassed by the Saxon race. There is now no part of the world that is open to Teutonic extension without encroaching to a corresponding degree upon those rights and sovereignty pre-empted by the Saxon.

The German Empire is less in area than the single State of Texas, while the Saxon race claims political dominion over one-half the landed surface of the earth and over all its ocean wastes. Yet the German Empire possesses a greater revenue than the American Republic, is the richest nation in productivity, and possesses a population 50 per cent. greater than the United Kingdom. Its actual military power is manifold greater than that of the entire Saxon race.

Germany is so tightly encircled by the Saxon race that it cannot make even a tentative extension of its territory or political sovereignty over non-Saxon states without endangering the integrity of the Saxon world. Germany cannot move against France without involving or including in its downfall that of the British Empire. It cannot move against Denmark on the north, Belgium and the Netherlands on the east, or Austria on the south, without involving the British nation in a final struggle for Saxon political existence. Any extension of German sovereignty over these non-British states predetermines the political dissolution of the British Empire. In a like manner any extension of Teutonic sovereignty in the Western Hemisphere, though against non-Saxon races and remote from the territorial integrity of the American Republic, can only succeed the destruction of American power in the Western Hemisphere.

The position in which Germany is now placed— the causes and responsibilities inherent in its position—is not new. Germany is not the first nation whose national activities have been circumscribed by powers weaker than itself, nor will it be the last. This is an old anomaly, and has a definite place in racial expansion. It precedes those epochal periods that mark the extinction of decadent states and the readjustment of the political world. The constancy of these causes and effects, the inevitability of their recurrence, regardless of time or geographical isolation, permits us to determine these facts with relative accuracy.

Unfortunately, it is customary for nations in their own time to deny the application of natural forces to their own activities. They believe that the hu-

man race moves forward in a straight line, instead
of in widening cycles, and that they have reached
a point where all that is past cannot affect them,
since they have created new conditions to which old
laws are not applicable. This assumption only
exemplifies the delusive character of the knowledge
they pretend to possess. Throughout all ages mankind has believed in this same directness of his
progress: that the human race would not again
come upon its own spoor. Yet we have not found
a single instance in modern times, either in the creation or extinction of political entities, that differs
in fundamental principles from those of ancient
eras.

Man is only wiser than those who have preceded
him in a wiser application of the laws that govern
his activities. The future relationship between the
Teutonic and the Saxon races is determined by five
conditions:

1. Whenever one nation, in the extension of its
sovereignty, is circumscribed and limited by another
nation, and at the same time possesses equal or
greater physical power, then the encompassing
nation is destroyed, since a state of equal or greater
military power occupying interior lines is as many
times stronger as there are political segments in
the circumscribed circle.

2. The elemental weakness of an encompassing
nation is that, being territorially vaster, it acts on
the defensive. This defense is not equal to, but is

less strong than, the defense of the strongest part. The weakness is proportionate to the number of entities composing the empire and the degree of their segregation.

3. The military power of the encompassing nation must always exceed that of the nation encircled in that proportion which insures the restriction of the theater of war to the territory of the encircled nation.

4. The subjugation of an encircled nation must be complete to result in victory to the encompassing nation. On the other hand, the defeat of a single segregated entity of the encompassing nation may result in the complete downfall of the whole.

5. In a struggle between nations situated as the Teutonic and the Saxon, the one whose preparation for war permits the seizure of the initiative insures to itself the probabilities of victory.

German expansion is made up of two distinct phases: the extension of German sovereignty or political control over non-Saxon states; the other by direct seizure of the British dominions. Heretofore we have only witnessed the extension of German sovereignty over the Teutonic states, an amalgamation in which is to be found the origin of the power that is forcing its way toward the dismemberment of the British Empire. Could England have prevented this amalgamation at a loss of one-half of her colonial possessions, it would have perpetuated the stability of British power more completely than any other sacrifice could have insured. When England yielded up the center of Europe to Germanic unity she lost the citadel of her European power.

Germany can eventually dissolve the British Empire by other means than the absorption, in one form or another, of continental Europe.

When one European state secures to itself that degree of the balance of power in Europe so that it cannot be affected by any coalition, inclusive of the British Empire, then British world sovereignty is at an end.

The duration of the British Empire rests primarily upon the preservation of the balance of power to Europe itself. It must struggle for this more than for its most valued possession, for upon it the integrity of all its possessions depends.

For England to preserve to herself the balance of power in Europe, it is necessary to limit the political and territorial expansion of any European state.

The amalgamation of Austria, the amalgamation of Italy were blows to British power; but when England permitted the amalgamation of the Germanic race it prepared the plans of its own sarcophagus.

Had Europe been divisible into no greater number of political entities during Napoleon's time than it is to-day, and had he exercised the same degree of power that he did at the beginning of the nineteenth century, the British Empire would have been dissolved subsequent to the Treaty of Tilsit.

When Germany completes the amalgamation of

those racial elements constituting the Teutonic power in Europe, the British Empire will find itself entirely without the sphere of European politics and incapable of forming a coalition against or assisting in the destruction of Germanic political and military institutions.

Germanic amalgamation has heretofore omitted three spheres — Denmark, the Netherlands, and Austria — that are strategically, politically, and economically more important to its world greatness than are all its other subsidiary states. Not until these have passed into the Germanic confederation will the world become cognizant of Germanic power.

Each of these spheres is as essential to the future of the German Empire as was Prussia necessary for the basis of Teutonic amalgamation. So vital are these states to Germanic expansion, and so inherent are the rights of the German race to their possession, that they can now be considered a portion of the empire in all but the alteration of their outward sovereignty; a change that will either just precede or occur concurrently with an Anglo-Saxon war, in the same manner as Schleswig-Holstein became part of the German nation, and the Austrian war preceded the Franco-Prussian conflict. In a war with Great Britain the occupation of Denmark and the Netherlands by Germany is just as necessary as was the occupation of Korea by Japan. They constitute German bases. Should British defense be capable of holding, by superior preparation and

initiative, the eastern frontiers of the Netherlands
and the southern frontiers of Denmark, the greatness of the British Empire goes down upon these
two undisputed theaters of war.

The absorption of Denmark by Germany is governed, not by German greed, but by natural forces.
The intensity of their application alone is influenced
by that racial avarice characteristic of the Teuton.
Controlling this assimilation, we establish the following conditions:

When a small state possesses territories that are
geographically part of a more powerful nation, the
exterritorial expansion of the latter is invariably
preceded by the absorption of the lesser state under
the following conditions:

1. When the small state is so placed strategically
that its possession is essential in the subsequent
wars of the greater.

2. When the small state is so placed geographically that its independence interferes with the
economic growth of the greater.

3. When the small state is so placed politically
that its absorption is essential to the greater nation
for the purposes of its political expansion.

4. When the people of the small state are racially
the same and are racially associated.

Denmark occupies one of the first places in the
strategic spheres of Europe, and is as essential to
Germanic power in the north of Europe as is the
possession of Gibraltar to the power of Great Britain

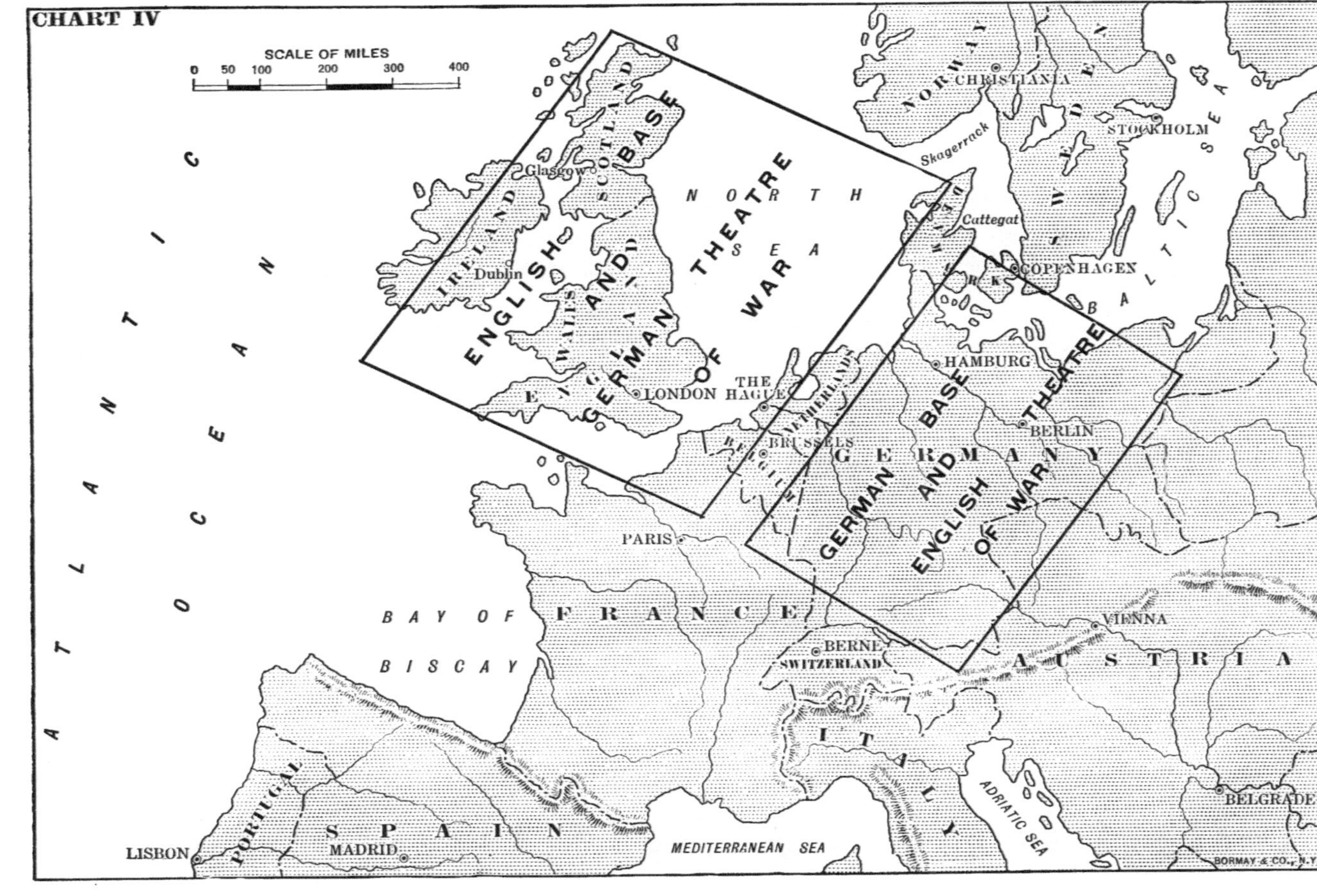

CHART IV
SCALE OF MILES
0   50   100   200   300   400
ATLANTIC OCEAN
NORTH SEA
ENGLISH BASE AND GERMAN THEATRE OF WAR
GERMAN BASE AND ENGLISH THEATRE OF WAR
IRELAND
Dublin
SCOTLAND
Glasgow
ENGLAND
WALES
LONDON
THE HAGUE
NETHERLANDS
BELGIUM
FRANCE
PARIS
HAMBURG
BERLIN
GERMANY
Skagerrack
Cattegat
COPENHAGEN
BALTIC SEA
NORWAY
CHRISTIANIA
SWEDEN
STOCKHOLM
DENMARK
SWITZERLAND
BERNE
VIENNA
AUSTRIA
ITALY
ADRIATIC SEA
BELGRADE
SPAIN
MADRID
PORTUGAL
LISBON
BAY OF BISCAY
MEDITERRANEAN SEA
BORMAY & CO., N.Y.

in the Mediterranean. Germany in her expansion must consider not alone the present, but the future, not so much the increases of her own wealth as the augmentation of those strategic places by which she can control the wealth and power of other nations, bringing about in due time those conditions upon which depend the future of the Teutonic race, the dissolution of the Anglo-Saxon Empire and the curtailment of the Russian.

Because of this duality of German progress the possession of those strategic positions that increase simultaneously her power over both empires constitutes a permanent basis upon which her future expansion must rest. In this category Denmark is more essential to the progress of German military power than any other single territory in this sphere.[1]

Denmark is the continuation of Germany. One might say that it is the thumb of the Teutons, by which she will crush the greatest of sea and land empires, leaving upon the world in this thumb-print the knowledge of her identity forever.

The value of the Netherlands to the German Empire is determined by the above laws, and not by the fact that its harbors give to Germany the opportunity of attack on the British Islands. The proximity of Holland to England does not constitute the true value of the Netherlands to Germany, which is twofold:

1. It is essential to the economic development of

[1] Chart IV.

western Germany and the amalgamation of the Teutonic races.

2. Its strategic value to Germany lies, not within, but outside, of Europe.

With the acquisition of Holland the German Empire expands simultaneously, not alone to the Western Hemisphere, but across the Pacific, securing a landed area three times greater than that of Germany and a native population equal to that of France. Germany becomes an Oriental empire, standing across the trade routes of eastern Asia and Europe and segregating Australasia to the solitudes of the southern Pacific.

We have already formulated in a previous work [1] certain laws governing naval expansion. These laws are as applicable to Germany as to any other empire:

1. The number of naval bases must be increased in proportionate ratio to the increase of the navy.

2. The efficiency of the navy is lessened whenever the number and capacity of naval bases is less than required by such fleets as conditions of warfare may force to base on them.

3. The possession of too few or not widely spaced bases means the restriction of naval activity to a defined, and perhaps unimportant, portion of the theater of war, as well as periods of complete inactivity consequent upon undue restriction.

4. The efficiency of the navy is correspondingly weakened where there are within such strategic

[1] *The Valor of Ignorance.*

triangles as are formed by two or three or more of its bases fortified positions belonging to the enemy.

By the operation of these laws it is apparent that in the extension of the German navy to an equality with that of Great Britain its utility is determined by a territorial expansion without Europe. Otherwise the sphere of its operations is confined to the North Sea. The effect of a navy upon the world and its trade is no greater than the radii of its operations.

At the time of the creation of the modern German navy one of three conditions was predetermined upon:

1. The absorption of the Netherlands and the utilization of her colonial possessions as naval bases.

2. The destruction of British naval supremacy, and the seizure of British oversea possessions as naval bases.

3. The absorption of the Netherlands and her colonial territories simultaneously with the destruction of British sea power and the seizure of her possessions.

It is in the acquisition of the colonial possessions of the Netherlands that rests the basic value of this kingdom to Germany. As the Dutch East Indies would establish German power in the Orient, so the Dutch possessions on the north coast of South America and the Dutch islands in the southern part of the Caribbean Sea permit what would be otherwise impossible—German naval activity in those regions. With the acquirement of the Dutch colonial possessions in the Western Hemisphere Germany enters upon her career to curtail, if not destroy, the nebulous sovereignty the Saxon race now imposes upon South America.

While the Monroe Doctrine forbids the acquisition of territory by European nations subsequent to its enunciation, it cannot interfere with Dutch sovereign rights, though the Dutch state becomes a part of the German Empire. This is the beginning of Teutonic sovereignty in the Western Hemisphere.

As the value of Holland to the German Empire lies without itself, so is it true of the extension of German sovereignty over Austria. It is not the twenty millions added to the German race or their territory that constitutes the value of Austria to Germany.

It lies in Asia Minor.

It belongs to the Mediterranean.

Already this Teutonic race, certain of its destiny, conscious of its strength, has stepped across the Bosphorus.

As Germany gains a sea by the occupation of Denmark, so Austria brings to her another. With the absorption of Austria the Mediterranean and its littoral passes within the environment of Berlin.

The destruction of Austrian sovereignty is the means to a great end. There is a savage sublimity in this thought—to use empires as stepping-stones.

BOOK II

All states are in perpetual war with all.   For that which we call peace is no more than merely a name, whilst in reality nature has set all communities in an unproclaimed but everlasting war with each other.—PLATO.

I

THE BRITISH EMPIRE AND THE WORLD

British Empire Subject to Same Laws as Others.—Not Immune from Attack.—Recession of Saxon along Original Lines of Expansion.—Military Expansion Not Arbitrarily Determined.—Japan's Special Sphere Pacific Ocean.—Development of Russia in Central Asia.—Preservation of Frontiers of Belgium, Holland, and Denmark Necessary.

WE have in the previous book examined into the relationship the Saxon race bears to the balance of the world, and have found it not what it is ordinarily supposed to be—an empire durable as the world itself—but one similar in its vulnerability to all other nations that have preceded it.

The instability of the British Empire is not due to the manner of its establishment, but to a subsequent denial of those immutable factors that determine not alone the formation of nations, but their progression and duration. The Saxon race, and those who from time to time directed its course, have with increasing frequency sought the greatness of the shadow for the durability of the substance. This Cheopian empire, built up by the old valor and genius of the race upon corners that were the four corners of the world, is now turned upon its apex.

149

Though its shadow lies upon more parts of the earth than ever heretofore, its durability rests, not upon the breadth of its base, but upon the strength of a single part. Toward this point, unhindered by the great shadow that falls upon them, the nations of the world are crowding; and when the last of the unsubstantial bastions are passed this great inverted pyramid of Saxon power will be cast down by the finger of some Cambyses, and, like Egyptian nationality, to remain in the midst of its own ruins, another monument of human vanity and credulity.

We have found in this examination that the old world in its vastness is gone. Oceans have become rivers, and kingdoms the environs of a single city. The solitudes of the earth have vanished, and the whole of the human race now struggles within a space no greater than was once allotted to a single empire. Small populations have become vast, and their hungers have grown, not proportionately to the increase of their numbers, but a thousandfold, more through the necessities of their civilization and the activity of their sciences.

Science has become the scavenger of the world. What once lasted mankind a generation is now consumed in a single day. And of what is left of Nature's resources the Saxon lays claim to seven-tenths. It is in consequence of these conditions that the races of the world are converging toward those resources under political dominion of the Saxon race. This convergence is not from nor toward widely separated spheres, but so jammed together are the races of the world that one hears the whisper of the other. Secrecy, like solitude, has abandoned mankind.

The British Empire owed its former immunity from attack and dissolution, not to its own power, but to the lack of power in others. This security departed with the advent of the era of mechanical invention, when science brought within the environs of Europe the most remote of British possessions and at the same time increased the necessity of European expansion. Convergent with the advent of these conditions the multiplicity of European kingdoms, upon which rested the basic element of Saxon safety, gave way through amalgamation to the present great powers, while in Asia, where for so many generations Saxon conquest had been unopposed, the dead have awakened and new empires have risen to dismay or destroy all that in Asia is left of Saxon power.

As it is more difficult to preserve to one's heirs that which has been gained during a lifetime than it is to secure it, so is this true with states. No individual spendthrift is more careless of his heritage than a nation, and none parts with it more freely than do those great empires whose power appears illimitable.

No receptacle is so shallow as the coffers of an heir.

The laws governing the contact of states, the

aggrandizement of one and the dissolution of the other through the convergence of their interests, and the wars that ensue from this convergence, have already been given.[1] By these we find that any contraction of the spheres within which nations contend for superiority increases the proximity and frequency of wars to the same degree as would follow from an increased acuteness of their angles of convergence. The significance of this to the British Empire is threefold. The world in a military sense is no larger than western Europe a hundred years ago. Its every portion comes within the military activity of a great state. The world is now a single theater of war; and in this theater, widely segregated, lies the Saxon Empire, claiming dominion over all its seas and more than half its lands, constituting the larger portion of those future theaters of war toward which all non-Saxon nations are converging. Innumerable conditions, changing from time to time, may alter their convergence, accelerate or retard the speed with which they advance; but there remains one constant factor that ever brings them nearer to the destruction of the British Empire and the absorption of its possessions—the progressive militant decadence of the Saxon. Whenever this decadence falls upon a race, as it has upon the Saxon, then the race not only ceases to advance, but recedes along the lines it originally traversed. The consequent convergence of surrounding nations

[1] *The Valor of Ignorance,* chap. iv, book i.

at once becomes acute, and their speed is accelerated in direct ratio to the increasing defenselessness of the decadent empire.

Nations never advance to their doom. They retreat to it.

While the British Empire is now, geographically, more vast than ever heretofore, its wealth and power, in a world sense, reached their maximum subsequent to the Napoleonic wars. National wealth and power are only relative. At that time there was no modern Germany nor France nor America nor Russia nor Japan. England was supreme, and in this supremacy, due rather to the weakness of others than to British strength, the militant decline of the nation began.

While some victories are the genesis of empires, some are their ruin, and in others germinate the causes of eventual decay.

Waterloo was a victory of this latter kind. It was the beginning of Germanic militant greatness and of Saxon militant decay.

At the close of the Napoleonic wars the elemental character of European economic wants and the remoteness from Europe of all British possessions permitted for a time a parallel progression of British and continental interests. The way to England's vast territories was by the sea, and that way the British sea power held secure. Toward the middle of the nineteenth century began not alone an alteration of political ideals in Europe, but the era of mechanical invention.   Each subsequent decade de-limited British security.

The steam-engine and the racial unification of Europe were the first enemies to British power.

Military expansion is not determined arbitrarily by legislation, but by conditions over which they have no control.   It is only by circumscribing these conditions endangering national security that a state can determine for itself the degree of its military expansion.   The exercise of such sovereignty, however, presupposes a dominant power over those states or conditions that might in their progress and development threaten Saxon supremacy.   Instead of Waterloo resulting in a declination of British militant expansion it should have been the beginning of a constant military growth not alone equal to the vulnerability of the Empire, consequent upon the segregation of its constituent parts, but to those greater dangers resulting from European racial amalgamation and the shrinkage of the world brought about by the constantly increasing efficiency of international communication and transportation.

Waterloo should have been an inspiration.   It became a memory.

To contemplate this memory is to shudder.

In the preceding book we have dealt specifically with those conditions productive of British dissolution as they exist in the Western Hemisphere, in Asia, in Europe, and upon the seas, showing that this tentative destruction is not the result of the old call of conquest upon the non-Saxon nations, but necessity forcing their expansion in direction of the greatest gain and upon lines of least resistance. By a strange fatality these lines coincide with those now being vacated by the retrocession of the Saxon race through the decay of its militant capacity, racial atrophy, and political dissolution.

In the entire world we have not found a single sphere toward which the expansion of other nations is directed that does not encroach upon the integrity of the British Empire, and to the extent that its disintegration goes on concurrently with each extension of their power. Up to the present time the movement of these nations has been restricted to those two phases of preparation that invariably precede all great wars and periods of conquest—internal consolidation and the establishment of extra-territorial spheres of restrictive aggrandizement. It can be considered as an historical maxim that no great power ever restricts to itself a sphere of special interest over a decadent state, except with the predetermination to eventually extend over it sovereign rights. Defeat alone averts this consummation. Whenever a decadent state, over which has been imposed restrictive rights or complete sovereignty, lies in the avenue of the conquering power's expansion, the adjoining state becomes subject to an identical fate if its capacity for defense is less than that of the expanding power.

In the growth and victories of Japan have been evolved in natural sequence the essential characteristics of this principle. The Pacific Ocean is Japan's sphere of special interest and aggrandizement. This is not an ambition. It is a necessity. It is forced upon Japan by the insular character of its empire, and by the action of certain natural laws which we now establish:

1. The security of an insular empire is determined, not by the defense of its own shores, but by the control of the coasts encompassing the sea in which it is situated.

2. Sea power in an insular empire is not measured by the number of its ships of war, but by its capacity to prevent the maritime superiority of any state placed on the external shores of the sea in which it is located. This capacity is primarily inherent not in naval but in military power.

3. Whenever a continental state abuts upon the sea in which is situated an insular kingdom, and acquires a relative equality in maritime power, the probabilities of eventual victory rest entirely with the continental nation.

Whenever the possibility of establishing Japanese sovereignty over the Pacific passes without the sphere of Japan's activity, the dissolution of that empire begins. In Japan the entire nation is intuitively cognizant of these laws, and because of them the Russian war was undertaken, not for the acquirement of continental possessions, but for the preservation of her maritime supremacy in northern Asia by the preclusion of Russia from the littoral of the Pacific.

It is the continuity of this progression and the maritime expansion of the Japanese Empire that now brings it into conflict with the Saxon race. Upon the success or failure of this struggle the future of Japan rests, and with the supremacy of that empire all that is Saxon in power and dominion departs from the Pacific.

In the middle East, in India, its seas and environs, we find the same essential principle directed against the tenure of the British race. As the Pacific, through the decay of Saxon militancy, has now become the sphere of Japanese expansion, so by this same lack of military progression those vast territories of the middle East have passed within the sphere of Russian conquest. Russia has not forced the Saxon from the frontiers of India, but has only followed slowly and unopposed along those avenues of expansion made possible by the retrocession of British power. The development of central Asia, bringing it within the environs of Greater Russia by the railroads that now traverse it—the tentative extension of Russian dominion over Persia—has all come within the character of peaceful internal development and consolidation. Yet it has also been, as we will hereafter show, the most complete and extensive preparation for the conquest of a definite reign ever undertaken in modern times.

In Europe, to a greater extent than in the Pacific

or Asia, has it become an established truism that all further territorial expansion is dependent upon the dissolution of the British Empire. In the amalgamation of minor European states British political domination over Europe came to an end. With the violation of England's Danish obligations and its military inability to preserve that nation's integrity, British power vanished utterly from the councils of European nations.

When England withdrew to the solitudes of her seas, it was not, as is ordinarily assumed, upon her own volition. She was forced upon these waste places of the world in the futile hope that power established there intervened between her possessions and those states in Europe with whom she could no longer contend. This was not an advance; it was a retreat, and one full of bitterness. Sea power has not had, nor can it have, any salient effect upon the internal political or military growth of continental states when their development is not dependent upon oceanic control. British sea power has done nothing to retard or prevent that unification and development of European power which, in due time, is to be directed to its own destruction. This prevention or diversion could alone be accomplished by the exercise of British military power within the continent itself. England has not until recent years become cognizant of the dangers that resulted from her failure to provide for a continuous expanding military establishment.

This is the old and pitiful blindness that comes upon nations, not from a lack of sight or knowledge, but from the intermittent fevers of their pride and credulity.

Ordinarily the readjustment of political and territorial boundaries proceeds concurrently with changes that occur in international political and economic relationship. But in the internal development and racial consolidation of Europe the readjustment of frontiers has been deferred. This alteration is now determinable solely by the utilization of the maximum military power of the strongest European nation. Whenever the disruption of old frontiers succeeds political consolidation these changes are not only marked by violence, but usher in those Napoleonic periods of warfare that fall, from time to time, upon this fretful world.

The excessive political and military development of a single nation or of a closely associated coalition of nations is now manifest in growth of Teutonic power and its ruthless entrance into the affairs of the world. The tentative establishment of German dominion in the past, not only over European states, but in the most distant parts of the world, is now about to give way to that consummation of sovereignty once exercised by Saxon elements.

In the modern extension of racial sovereignty the expenditure of physical power is directed, not against the minor states intended to be absorbed, but toward the greatest power concerned in the preservation of their integrity and independence. When that power is destroyed they fall, quite naturally, within the domain of the conqueror, as shown in the absorption of Korea by Japan.

To absorb Belgium, Holland, and Denmark, it is necessary that Germany destroy England.

It is the British Empire, more than all the other powers, that is involved in every manifestation of German expansion. While the Saxon race and its possessions on every continent constitute the foci of the convergent interests of all other nations, German expansion embodies in a single concrete expression all these diverse interests, since its convergence is not upon the frontiers of the British Empire, but upon the very center of it. The anomalous condition of Teutonic progression, however, permits the Saxon race to conceal from itself the dangers and disasters it involves. The Saxon has seized upon this self-deception with that eagerness peculiar to peoples militarily decadent.

As Prussia's seizure of Schleswig-Holstein ended the period when England gave down the law to Europe and shaped the destinies of its innumerable states, so its continued military decadence has led to its ejection from the councils of those nations. A new period, even more portentous than the preceding, has now made its appearance. While the annexation of the Danish Duchies betrayed the weakness and falsity of British military policy, so the extension of Germanic sovereignty to either

Denmark or the Netherlands or Belgium will result in the final elimination of England from European affairs.

The failure of England to realize a half-century ago that the southern frontiers of Denmark were her frontiers, and that her inability to defend them must subsequently result disastrously to her integrity, now bears its bitter fruit in forcing upon her an identical but greater necessity of defending, not alone the present frontiers of Denmark, but the eastern frontiers of the Netherlands and Belgium. Should this inexorable obligation be met with the same national defalcation and military bankruptcy as was the case a half-century ago, then the penalty will not alone be Saxon ejection from Europe, but the eventual dissolution of their Empire.

Throughout the preceding book we confined ourselves to the consideration of basic dangers that threaten Saxon survival in every portion of the world. In this inquiry we put aside all ephemeral conditions and difficulties such as appear to impede and endanger the Empire's existence. We have taken into account only those elemental influences and principles that determine in all ages the duration and extinction of nations. The futurity of the British Empire has been considered only in its entirety—in its relation to the natural destiny of political existence, and the tragic phenomena that record its rise and decline. Its destiny is marked, as that of other empires, in the ever-recurring tides of national virility and decay, in the flood and ebb of human greatness.

The British Empire, as well as all others that have preceded it, betray characteristics peculiar to each. It is these characteristics, varying from generation to generation, that lead nations to deceive themselves in the belief that their progress is alone wise and their government imperishable. These passing singularities, marking only the transient idealities of successive periods, we have excluded from consideration, restricting ourselves to those principles that are constant in their application through every age and over every race.

God has not transgressed these laws, and His people have gone the same way as those who knew nothing of Him or His decrees.

That finality upon the brink of which the British Empire now hesitates, perhaps for no more than a moment of time, is or is not an immediate consummation only as the Empire accepts or continues to deny those principles which the progression and dissolution of nations have established.

It is now that we turn from the contemplation of the Empire and the perils that are coexistent with its vastness to the consideration of the causes that have been productive of these dangers. As in the preceding book, we will consider only those conditions that are universal in their effect upon its security. Removed, as we are, far from the ringside of party politics, with its pitiful aspirations and small bruised noses, we will view these causes of Saxon decadence without prejudice or bitterness, though not without sorrow, as we witness what is perhaps destined to be the final passage of this vast Empire.

II

LIMITATIONS OF NAVAL WARFARE

National Ideals.—Principles Governing Army and Navy in Hostilities.—Navy of an Insular and Army of a Continental Power Determine Expansion of Opponent.—Naval and Land Warfare. —Disaster in War Result from Victory as well as Defeat.— Kinds and Degrees of Battle.—Lines of Communication.

NATIONAL ideals are of two kinds—the present and the historic. By their character and the degree of influence they exercise upon the nation are we able to determine, in a certain sense, the direction of its progression.

When national ideals are divorced from the historic and belong wholly to the present, as those based upon party politics or political expedients, they are as transitory as the conditions that give them birth. National decadence then proceeds in inverse ratio to the increased dominance of these ideals over national policy.

When national ideals are the unused products of events existent only in an historical sense, there results an inflexibility of governmental progression that culminates in national atrophy and decay.

When national ideals are derived from those historic events productive of the state's maximum greatness, and constitute the principles directing present ideals, there results a truer association of the past with the present. So long as this continues national ideals cease to be either transient or atrophied, but, maintaining the state at its relative maximum power, are coexistent with it.

When national ideals are founded upon conditions no longer existent yet maintained under the delusion of their immutability, they become not a possible but an actual cause of national dissolution.

It is in relation to these last ideals, as they affect the Saxon race, that we are to consider the false interpretation now given to the old ideals of British sea power, the unreality of its permanence under existent conditions, and the limitations of its functions.

Sea power is not an entity. It is not self-existent nor absolute, but remains constant in its subordination to numerous basic conditions that determine, from time to time, the rise, duration, and decline of nations situated within or upon the environs of the sea.

Sea power is the exercise of physical force in that specific theater of war where national welfare necessitates its use in varying degrees of potentiality. It differs only in the means of its application from conflicts waged on land. Those principles that govern the empire in its extension or defense remain constant, whether the struggle is by land or by sea. Fleets, as armies, are but the agencies of nations when their activities pass from peace to war. As the purposes of a campaign, the character of the theater of war and the objective to be attained specify the greater or lesser use of cavalry or infantry or artillery, so do the general conditions of war and the ultimate objective of the struggle determine the relative significance of the main combative elements of the belligerents, the army or the navy. In a general sense these are governed by three principles:

1. In a war between two insular powers the navy constitutes the arm of supreme importance.

2. In a war between two continental powers the army constitutes the arm of supreme importance.

3. In a war between an insular power and a continental nation a superior navy plus a relative equality of land forces constitutes the true proportion of the two arms.

The first two principles are self-evident, but in the third we find the development of British militant power to fulfil but one of these conditions. The results, as we will show in this and subsequent chapters, is the nullification of its naval power by the inadequacy of its land forces when engaged in war with an equally great continental nation. In such a conflict the naval power of the insular nation determines the degree of naval superiority or equality necessary to the continental state to enter upon the struggle, but the land forces of the continental nation plus the defensive works intervening between its vital center and the seaboard designate the degree of military strength necessary to the insular power.

The navy of an insular power defines the expansion of its continental opponent, while the land forces of the continental power determine the military expansion of its insular opponent.

Between naval and land warfare there exist inherent differences that, as yet, human progress has not altered. The causes and purposes of war, the relative strength or weakness of the combatants, define the theaters of war, while the peculiarities of these theaters determine the manner and characteristics of its conduct. If the conflict is between an insular and a continental state, the sea becomes the first area of the struggle. If the insular power suffers defeat, its war is at an end, since a land defense by an insular nation against a continental power in command of the sea is a political, military, and economic impossibility.

If the naval power of the continental nation is destroyed, it results only in a transfer of the theater of war from the sea to the land, from naval to land forces, since a continental state with land frontiers is economically free from the insular nation's control of the sea. Its military forces must be defeated before its internal economies or political powers are affected to the extent of suing for peace. In the recent war between Russia, a continental state, and Japan, an insular nation, this principle is made clear. Had Russia destroyed the naval forces of Japan the war would have ended on the date of that disaster.

It is not necessary, in modern times, to invade an insular state to destroy it.

The naval victory remaining to Japan, the insular nation, resulted only in a transfer of the theater of war from the sea to the land, giving to Japan no more than a comparative equality with Russia, but rendering secure her line of communication. Had Japan's navy been a hundredfold greater and her land forces inferior in numbers or constitution to those of Russia, the dreadful dramas of her seas would have marked rather the end than the beginning of her greatness.

Japan's navy and its use during this war show the true and limited functions of naval warfare as employed by an insular nation against a continental power. It is defensive (1) to prevent the continental state from gaining command of the sea; (2) to safeguard the future lines of communication between the insular state and the continental, to which is transferred the theater of combat subsequent to the naval victory of the insular power.

It is impossible to determine with exactitude the conduct of a future conflict or to apply to it with any degree of certainty the experiences of a previous war. To define, therefore, the relative importance of naval and land warfare other than by the general principles just laid down is impracticable, since the means and utensils of war are never identical in any two periods of time. Yet the laws governing the military preparation of an insular power against a continental nation, and the naval preparation of the latter against an insular kingdom, remain constant to all such nations, and identical in all periods of time, whether the ships of war are the wooden triremes or the most thunderous of dreadnoughts, whether the soldiers are spear and pike men or the engineers of the destructive forces now made use of.

The violation of the above principles is due sometimes to the ignorance of civilians, who, in all nations, are largely responsible for the development or deterioration of naval power; sometimes to erroneous interpretation by naval and military authorities. The failure to rightly understand these principles results in that anomalous state of affairs whereby naval expansion is controlled by conditions far removed from those laws that should govern its development.

In proportion as the maritime interests of a nation increase so does the necessity for naval expansion make itself felt. It is at this point that insular nations err. Almost invariably they regard this necessity of naval increase from the defensive viewpoint; yet the danger they would guard against does not originate in nor belong to the sea. It is inherent in the political domination of another state whose interests are convergent with those of the insular nation.

A successful defense of an insular kingdom leaves that kingdom worse off than before the attack. The power of the continental state remains constant, while the angle of convergence originating in the nation itself is not altered. Only the speed of its movement has been retarded, and this but in proportion to its remedial naval losses. Unless the insular nation is now in position, as was Japan, to utilize her security by sea to assume the offensive and accept the transfer of the theater of war to the territories of the enemy, its naval victory is without value. The result would be, in modern times, no more than an armistice, a dreadful procrastination in which insular nations are the first to consume themselves.

Because of this misconception and failure to realize that the only objective of war is to destroy the enemy's capacity to wage it, there has been brought about in insular kingdoms the expansion of naval power to the neglect of the land forces. Yet in a war with a continental nation the navy can do no more than protect its oceanic lines of communication. Victory can only be gained by use of armies.

To a similar misconception is due the corollary of this fatal error, that the safety of insular kingdoms is the consequence of their own power as derived from the security of the sea, whereas it has been due to the non-naval expansion of continental states.

The purpose of war is to destroy the enemy's resources or the government controlling them. It is this savage simplicity that bewilders nations and plunges them into the fatal maze of evasion and conjecture, from which, to a militarily decadent state, there is no exit.

Disasters in war result from victory as well as defeat. There are three kinds and degrees of battle:

1. The battle that makes possible a definite advance and insures protection to lines of communication, as Vicksburg and Leipsic.

2. The defeat of armies to the extent of rendering possible the destruction of their resources or the seizure of their governments, as Wagram and Jena.

3. The destruction of the enemy's resources or the seizure of its government, as Arbela and Sedan.

The first of these battles belongs to the beginning of a war, the second to its progression, and the last to its culmination.

A naval battle, with one exception, belongs to the first subordinate class of tactical conflict, the sole purpose of which is to interrupt or protect definite lines of communication. A victory has only the relative effect of an interrupted or protected line, the significance of which depends upon the value of the communication. This value has three gradations:

1. It reaches its maximum importance when the war is between insular nations; then the complete interruption of these lines results in victory to the nation controlling the sea.

2. It is least important when the war is between continental powers of the same sphere, since their vital theaters of war are not maritime and their lines of communication are restricted to land.

3. When a war is between a continental and an insular power the effect of victory is vital only as regards the insular nation. As in a war between Germany and the British Empire, the destruction of the British fleet is followed by a complete severance of its lines of communication and its downfall. The destruction of the German fleets, on the other hand, results only in a return to conditions existent prior to the war, unless the Empire possesses, as did Japan, land forces capable of resuming the combat on the land theater to which the enemy has retired.

III

Conditions that Determined Saxon Suzerainty Now Changed.—
Inadequacy of British Navy.—Reduction of Distance Increases
Convergence of International Interests.—Sea Power in an Insular
Empire Not Measured by Ships of War.—Struggle of All Great
Continental Nations for Control of the Sea.—Preliminary De-
struction of British Empire Confined to Peace.

WHEN the causes productive of certain conditions diminish in number or potentiality, the
resultant conditions lose their corresponding significance. If the same factors that made possible the
British Empire were still existent, and its sea power
constant in its superiority, the dominion of the
Saxon over the world would continue undisputed.
But, of these five coexistent conditions that once
determined Saxon suzerainty over the earth, all
have passed away or have been merged imperceptibly into a new aspect.

1. The absence in Europe from the sixteenth to
the middle of the nineteenth century of any nation
possessing power or capacity to compete with the
Saxon for the possession of the sea and newly discovered world. There was no Russian Empire,
nor German, nor Austrian, nor Italian. The de-

173

cline of the Portuguese, the Spanish, the Dutch, and the French left the Saxon supreme. Upon the collective wreckage of these latter nations, at a time when the primitive world made it possible, the British Empire was established.

2. The world outside of Europe presented at this formative period two phases peculiarly favorable for the extension of British power—(a) the tribal character of the races of the Western Hemisphere and its great natural resources; (b) the military and political impotence of the great nations occupying Asia.

3. The geographical situation of the Western Hemisphere, the islands of the seas, the Levant, and the Orient, in relation to Europe, with which intercommunication was restricted to the sea.

4. The strategic position of the British Islands so placed before the oceanic exit of Europe that if Europe going out upon the sea was not directly forbidden the result was indirectly the same, since these British Islands severed all European lines of oceanic communication at their most vital point—that of their convergence and dispersion. As an island fortress placed in the center of a waterway commands, on all sides, the entrance to a harbor, so England, in a larger sense, was placed before Europe.

5. The extremities of British sea power have heretofore rested upon those parts of the world devoid of naval strength. The Atlantic radii terminated

in the sparsely inhabited regions of the Western Hemisphere and the wastes of the south coast of Africa. The radii of the Indian Ocean ended in India and the uninhabited islands of the Indian Ocean. The Pacific radii terminated in the exhausted civilization of east Asia and in barren or savage islands. The power that might affect British command of the sea was relegated to Europe, and was there aborted in its inception.

All of these conditions have changed. The western Atlantic, where once the radii of British naval power rested upon the security of savage solitudes, is now patrolled by great navies politically and militarily alien to British supremacy. In the eastern Atlantic, in the environs of the seas where is situated the base of the Empire, are other alien powers approaching a naval equality with that of Britain and reversing those former conditions that made possible British naval supremacy. Europe now threatens the radii of British naval power at their inception, while the naval expansion of Mediterranean powers, once non-existent, severs the main line connecting the center of the Empire with its termini in the Pacific. In that vast ocean, as in the Atlantic, those solitudes which were once the exterior bases of British naval power now no longer exist. The American republics dominate the eastern Pacific as they do the western Atlantic, while the western Pacific has passed under the naval dominion of an Asian nation.

Heretofore British naval supremacy has depended upon the maintenance of its superiority by the control of two localities—the west coast of Europe, adjacent to the British Islands, and the Mediterranean. So long as these two theaters of maritime war were mastered all exterior seas were subject to British control.

The effectiveness of this early sea power resulted not so much from its combative pre-eminence as from its political absolutism, its freedom from international control and restriction. But as old conditions passed away the absolute character of its dominion over vast unfrequented seas disappeared before the rise of great nations in the west and east. Then the restriction of insular maritime prerogatives by international interference followed and have altered, in their e. pression, the principles that once conserved British sea power.

The simultaneous development of naval power in Europe, the Mediterranean, the western Atlantic, the eastern Atlantic, and the Pacific has resulted in this portentous state of affairs, that, while the naval expansion of European states approaches a naval equality with the total British maritime forces, the Empire's exterior bases and their lines of communication are already dominated by alien navies to the extent that only a withdrawal of the main fleets from the defense of the United Kingdom can diminish the naval supremacy of these distant nations in their respective seas.

The inadequacy of the British navy is due not alone to a lack of corresponding military power, but to the policy of arbitrarily determining its expansion by the formula of the European two-power maxim, when its development must alone be determined by dangers threatening the Empire as a whole—her exterior lines and bases as well as the interior.

As the theater of war is distant from the United Kingdom and approaches the main base of the enemy the Empire's naval capacity, regardless of numerical superiority, decreases proportionately. Because of this principle the danger of foreign naval expansion in distant seas increases in constant progression. Moreover, as the naval power of a nation situated on the exterior lines and bases of the Empire is augmented the insecurity of the interior lines increases in proportion, regardless of European naval growth. When, therefore, British naval power is reduced to the state that it is incapable of protecting its exterior lines and bases simultaneously with the defense of its interior lines, the end is at hand. The complexity of modern international relationship is such that it demands the simultaneous defense of two or more frontiers. This necessity is especially true of the British Empire, because of the constant convergence of all nations toward those dominions and interests incorporated in the Empire.

The area of an ocean is never the same during any two periods of time. As human intelligence progresses its vastness diminishes. In ancient times the oceans merged into and were part of the Infinite. Only gods traversed them. Man has now pilfered what these gods once possessed. He has looted Olympus. He whispers across oceans. His voice is heard in its depths, his cries overhead. Yet he is unconscious of the limitations of his thievery.

When the seas shrink the means assuring their control must be increased.

The lessening significance of sea control, as divorced from political domination and military power, is due to conditions heretofore not experienced by the human race. These are reducible to two general phases. The progression of mechanical invention, whereby the curtailment of distance has so altered or destroyed old military limitations that their laws and axioms are now useless.

To reduce distance is to increase the convergence of international interests. To diminish space, geographical and political, is to merge small states into greater units. This passage is war. This unification conflict. Mankind, like metals, is welded together by fire and by blows.

When communicable means are increased in number, capacity, and speed, the world undergoes a corresponding shrinkage. In the process of this contraction there results a greater intensity in political expansion, a corresponding development of military capacity to wage war. The delimitation of distance by science, in its relationship to warfare, is nowhere more emphatic than upon the seas, or more decisive in its effects.

The decrease of oceanic space lessens proportionately the power of insular nations to command the seas.

During the preinventive age the dominion of the oceans fell to insular states, because their national evolution depended primarily upon their oceanic expansion. The reverse of this condition determined the expansion of continental states, their extension of empire being almost invariably restricted to land. The sea is only a means to an end. In its entirety it is no more than a desert across which pass the highways of the world. Heretofore it was not necessary for continental nations to traverse them, since their immediate resources not only exceeded the demand, but their production involved less labor and less time and less risk than was alone involved in crossing the half-known ocean wastes.

Insular nations, on the other hand, were obliged to cross seas not only on account of the limitations of their resources, but because the first outward movement involved the sea. The necessity of its mastery increased concurrently with the necessity of insular expansion.

Science has now not only reduced the passage of seas from months to days and brought all nations into competition for these highways, but it has so augmented the hunger of all peoples, continental as well as insular, that the possession of the undeveloped resources of the world is essential to their progression and survival.

The more vast the oceans were, as due to the limited ability to cross them, the more were they given over to the undisputed dominion of insular powers. When, however, the economic necessity of continental nations forced them overseas at a time when science had abridged oceanic vastness so that to cross the seas was not relatively longer than to pass their land frontiers, they entered into competition for their possession. It is this struggle with which we are now concerned.

When the supremacy of insular nations is alone dependent upon maritime strength, it is soon destroyed.

In the ruins of Carthage is to be found the epitome of this credulity.

We have already shown that the security of an insular empire is determined, not by the defense of its own shores, but by the control of the coasts encompassing the sea in which it is situated. This defense must necessarily be, in many instances, military rather than naval. Continental nations now competing with the Saxon for the control of the seas are all converging upon the British Empire, since a passage from their shores to the seas is an infringement of the dominions of this insular nation.

Sea power in an insular empire is not measured by its ships of war, but solely by its capacity to prevent military superiority in any state placed upon the external shores of the sea in which it is located. This capacity is primarily inherent not in naval but in military power. Whenever a continental state abuts upon the sea in which is situated an insular kingdom and acquires a relative equality in maritime power, the probabilities of eventual victory rest entirely with the continental nation.

In the loose, irresponsible way by which man defines conditions are we to look for that endless, depthless bog that swallows up so much of his tentative wisdom, and in due time his empires and his gods. To this error in definition we must attribute the present misconception of the term "control of the sea." This only means the control of the sea for the purpose of attacking or defending lands segregated by oceanic space. When, however, an attack upon these territories is equally feasible by land frontiers, then the "control of the sea" becomes no more than a hopeless, delusive phrase. The importance of sea control to military enterprise is only as a safe means of communication between theaters of war separated by oceanic space. The value of the mastery of these lines is determined, not on account of the lines *per se*, but the worth of the territories at both ends and the degree of power exercised over these lands by the possession of their sea-lines of communication. Prior to this mechanical age the control of the sea determined the political and economic supremacy of sea power and its mastery over all lands dependent upon it. With the increasing utilization of mechanical inventions, as applied to locomotion and communication, the sea-lines lost their exclusive significance while land-lines of international communication increased in importance. To-day European intercommunication is by land rather than by sea. Europe moves on Asia, Russia on India and the extreme Orient, by land instead of, as formerly, by sea. To-morrow all of Asia and Africa, as well as the Western Hemisphere, will be included in this alternate route by which continental nations may extend their sovereignty over the weaker states of their continents indifferent to the activity of naval power as exercised by insular kingdoms.

It is at this point that we are brought to the contemplation of a strange and, for insular nations, portentous anomaly—the simultaneous struggle of all great continental powers to secure maritime supremacy not only in their adjacent seas, but over the world. This is not due to the old principles of insular sea power, but is the result of economic problems applied to old continental nations impelling them toward the resources of unexploited continents.

The shrinkage of oceanic space has, by bringing continental nations into closer contact, decreased insular significance and increased the universality and intensity of continental struggles and the necessity to secure control of the intervening sea-lines whose distance diminishes with each inventive decade.

As the seas grow smaller in their traversible time, their control by insular nations lessens in almost exact proportion. These two simultaneous though diametric movements result in a third, the irruption of continental states upon the sea without a diminution of their military capacity to expand or defend themselves by land.

It is through this trinitation made possible by human progress that the power of insular kingdoms grows less and less. The diminution of insular naval power is not the result of war. It is the work of peace; a progression toward continental supremacy instead of insular. This movement is not apparent in peace. It only manifests itself in war in greater or lesser degree according to the significance of the combatants.

The preliminary destruction of British supremacy is confined to peace, and is inherent in four ante-bellum conditions, two positive and two negative:

1. The increasing economic independence of continental states from insular command of the sea.

2. The increasing political dominance of continental states in determining the character of international naval restrictions and immunities.

1. The increasing economic dependence of insular kingdoms upon continental productions.

2. The decreasing power of insular nations in international tribunals where ordinances regulating naval warfare are formulated.

There are in the world only two insular empires;

all other states are continental. In international conferences where declarations are made and agreed to for the regulation of international peace and war those laws favorable to the continuance of insular supremacy upon the seas and correspondingly detri- . mental to the extension of continental sea power diminish as the numerical disproportion between continental and insular nations increases.

Because of this fatal growth of continental power over international conferences, we witness at each of these congresses a diminution of those naval prerogatives that constitute the essential principles of insular power and survival. This determination, on the part of the greater continental states, to deprive sea nations in the time of peace of their peculiar advantages to wage naval war will continue until the continental states secure their approximate elimination from the international regulations of maritime war.

These changes will be economic rather than military, since naval war is not a decisive factor when waged between an insular and a continental state. It is basically restricted to the preservation of the economic freedom of belligerents. Continental powers will, therefore, insist upon the limitation of neutral shipping and an extension of the contraband of war. When they extend the contraband to include necessities vital to the life of a nation, as food-stuffs, and at the same time limit the neutrality of shipping to the degree that neutral vessels conveying these necessities to the ports of either belligerent are subject to capture and destruction, the capacity of an insular nation to wage war on a basis of equality ends.

An insular state has no neutral frontiers.

Every port of entry belonging to a continental state, except on the seaboard, is neutral.

Modern economic conditions are now universal in the production and the demand of human necessities. This economic universality, together with the development of overland transportation, renders continental nations, with their neutral land frontiers, immune from the activity of such maritime laws. Its only effect in oversea products is an overland transshipment through the territories of an adjacent neutral state.

In this dreadful, silent conflict of peace we witness the first crumbling-away of Saxon naval power.

IV

SAXON STRUGGLE FOR SURVIVAL—RUSSIA

National Greatness Based on Political Future.—Principles Prescribing Naval Activity.—Principles Governing Probabilities of Victory or Defeat in War.—Power Exercised Through Control of Sea Decreases as Overland Communication Increases.—Navy Useless in Attack on India by Russia.—Laws Governing Defense of India.

THE destruction of an empire precedes the war that wrecks it. Such a war is not the cause; it is only the culmination of national ruin, the conflagration and wild clamor that mark its end.

Disastrous wars are the failures of peace.

One must look to the peace that preceded an international struggle to determine its issue, and never to the war itself. This error in failing to differentiate between real and apparent causes leads nations to trust themselves to the luck of war. Yet cause and effect are not dice, nor natural laws a game of chance.

God does not gamble.

The defense of a nation, like its progression, is determined by conditions over which national desire or character have no mastery. While social progression is as flexible as its evolution is rapid, military transition is governed by no such impulsion. Its inflexibility increases, instead of disappearing, with each augmentation of militant decadence. The failure to acknowledge the mutability of governmental institutions is the constant recurring cause of national dissolution.

To prevent national decadence due to the militant indifference of its military character constitutes the first elements of a nation's defense. To prevent the expansion of those nations whose interests are convergent is the second. These are correlative and basic conditions upon which depends national security, and which the Saxon has within the last decade abandoned.

As the eventual destruction of an empire is determined by the militant expansion of surrounding states plus its own recession, the first principle of defense is to stop, not only the retrogression of the empire, but the corresponding extension of those states whose political and geographical interests are or may become convergent. The ability of British naval power alone to accomplish this has been brought to an end.

The political and geographical expansion of other nations is now taking place in direct ratio to, not the present, but the eventual shrinkage or dissolution of the British Empire.

National greatness is based upon the political future; decadence upon the present; destruction upon the past.

The elements that now constitute the basis of British Imperial defense are the antitheses of those conditions that brought about its creation. The determinate factors of that period necessitated a great navy supplemented only by inferior land forces. Now, however, the maintenance and progress of the Empire is conditioned by the salient characteristics of this era, and not those of three hundred years ago.

There is no security for a nation constituted as the British Empire, except in the positive prohibition of convergent expansion on the part of other nations. At one time this was accomplished by the British navy, and so long as the principal means of international association and intercourse were restricted to and by the sea through the inadequacy of overland transportation, any tentative extension of political power inimical to British supremacy was circumscribed by its naval forces. Had not land intercommunication progressed to the point it has now attained, or were all nations insular, the supremacy of the British navy would still maintain its old mastery over the world.

The reversal of the burden of war to the land forces of the Empire is due to the inability of its naval forces to retard the expansion of those nations whose growth can only take place at the expense or destruction of the Empire. The elimination of British sovereignty from the Western Hemisphere; the expansion of Asiatic nations; the extension of Germanic power in Europe and Asia Minor; the passage of Russian sovereignty over Persia and India are, as we will hereafter show, in no way concerned with the power of the British navy.

As we now pass from the consideration of principles that prescribe the limitation of British naval activity to their application, we will restrict our examination of these changes to two extremes:

1. Imperial dissolution due to the seizure or the destruction of its base.

2. Imperial dissolution through the invasion and shrinkage of its most remote frontiers.

It is by showing, in these two extreme theaters of war, the uselessness of naval power alone to preserve the integrity of the Empire, that we establish the invariability of these principles in all intermediate theaters governed by the same conditions. We have heretofore laid down as laws certain modern factors that control the means and conduct of war between insular and continental states. These conditions are not new. They are as old as war itself. It is their transmutation through the medium of modern science that makes them appear strange and unreasonable to the human mind. It is because of man's adherence to established customs and his unwillingness to depart from the ideals of his forefathers that we are conscious of his inability to accept these principles, though evolved out of his old labors and triumphs and disasters. Because of this refusal he continues to build up his empires, only to dwell in their ruins.

We know, from the study of peace conditions preceding the extinction of great empires, the cause that led to their dissolution. We know, moreover, that the acquisition of such knowledge was possible to these nations prior to their destruction. But, owing to the fact that a nation is never more vain of its strength than on the eve of destruction, this knowledge passes with their vanity into the slag and cinders of their ruin.

We cannot foretell the conduct of future wars conditioned by transient elements—the expedients of man and time and place—but we are able to determine the consummation of definite struggles within specific theaters of war by ascertaining during the peace that precedes the conflict the basic factors that constitute, in the final quotient, victory or defeat. These are reducible to three principles:

1. When the preparations of two belligerents, during the preceding peace, are opposed, one hastening away from and the other toward war, the probabilities of victory belong to the warlike nation in proportion to the influence their respective inclinations exercise over the ideals of the state. This is so absolute that history has recorded no exception.

2. When identical victories have not identical results, but possess different values to each belligerent, then the probabilities of final success belong to that belligerent whose strategic and military advantages give to his victories a maximum value. This is applicable to the military relationship exist-

ing between Germany and the British Empire. A British naval victory only transfers the theater of war from the sea to the land; a German victory destroys the Empire.

3. When the forces of one belligerent are incapable of acting against the forces of the other in the determinate theater of war because of its composition, then victory goes to the combatant who possesses that capacity. In a war between England and Russia, if the decisive theater is the sea, we are cognizant of British victory; but if the area of combat upon which the war is to be ultimately decided is Persia and India, the inutility of the navy is apparent.

When we ascertain, under varying conditions, what is the maximum power necessary to assure victory and then gain that power, we are able to determine not only the means to the end, but the end itself. Russia, failing to estimate the power necessary to conquer Japan, was herself defeated. Japan, on the other hand, judged differently. She did not commit herself to the erroneous belief which now enmeshes the British Empire—the belief that naval victory constitutes final success. Japan, measuring with exactitude the limitations and specific functions of her navy, built up her land forces to that degree of power plus strategic advantages that would insure to her the probabilities of victory.

The failure of the Saxon race to realize the limitations of naval force under modern conditions is primarily due to the decadence of military comprehension. A nation's mentality is no more than the composite mentality of the individuals that compose it. The degree of acuteness in judging the complex conditions that its progression involves is determined by the mental characteristics predominant in its population. The viewpoint of a tradesman is not that of a soldier; that of a soldier not the same as a lawyer. Acuteness and exactitude in judgment are the result of their respective mental environment, training, and inclination. This is equally true of the nation's composite mind circumscribing its perception and judgment to the specific character determined by popular inclination.

The national mind of Japan is militant. Its comprehension is correspondingly acute and exact in the military phase of human progress. The modern British mind, on the other hand, had substituted the pre-eminence of the individual for that of the state and the evasiveness of the legal mind for the perception of the soldier. Brilliancy is reduced to individual achievement. The power and grandeur of the state disintegrate, and the nation enters upon an era of self-deception. In this condition of national fraud military perception departs from the common mind, leaving only to a minority that old militant omniscience which makes possible the survival of a race.

Militancy is the palladium God gives once to each race. It is His token of their equality.

The military judgment of a non-militant public mind is worthless. This is evident in the divergent judgments of the Japanese and British nations relative to the modern defense and progression of their respective empires. Both are insular, and both are confronted by identic conditions. The Japanese recognize the true functions and limitations of naval power; the Saxons do not.

For an insular kingdom to understand those modern conditions that impose upon it the expansion of its naval forces, and yet at the same time circumscribe its maritime power, is to understand a paradox only intelligible to the composite intuition of a militant state. It is incomprehensible to the popular mind of a commercial state.

This paradox is composed of two principles:

1. As continental states in their expansion pass without the maritime control of insular nations, the more essential does the control of the sea become to island kingdoms, since their naval power passes from the offensive to the defensive.

The defeat of an offensive movement is retardation. The defeat of a defensive position is disaster.

2. The command of the sea means, not the sea, but the nations situated upon its shores. It means the control of their lines of communication and the segregation of one nation from another to the advantage of the dominant sea power.

As overland lines of international communication increase in number and length and efficiency, the power exercised through the control of sea-routes diminishes proportionately. Once it was necessary for European states to approach the world by the sea. England, in command of the sea, circumscribed and conditioned their activities.

Europe now moves upon Asia and Africa by land, not by sea. The United States, at one time subject to the British control of the Atlantic, now moves up and down the Western Hemisphere by rail.

Until recently Russian movement in force against the Far East and India was restricted to the sea. So long as England continued in control of the sea-routes to India and the Pacific, these theaters of expansion and war were without the sphere of Russia. Now all is changed. The sea power of the British Empire has no longer any effect upon the expansion of Russia in eastern Asia, nor her advance upon Persia and India.

Unless the forces of a nation possess specific and decisive power in one or more of the three phases of war—the strategic, the economic, and the combative—then those forces are useless, and the nation must secure other ways and other means of conducting war.

It is in the examination of these three phases of international struggle that we discover the uselessness of the British navy as a means to prevent the conquest of India and Persia or the expansion of Russia in eastern Asia.

The strategic prohibition of the British navy

from a participation in this conflict is due to a single fact—the sea does not intervene between Russia and the extreme limits of her future conquests. In no place does the Russian advance come in contact with the sea, except at the conclusion of her expansion on the seaboard of eastern Asia, Persia, Asia Minor, or India. Only when Russia, completing her conquest of these regions, attempts to dominate the Pacific or Indian Ocean with her naval forces do the British fleets become a factor in the struggle.

The inability of the British navy to prevent the destruction of the Empire east of the Suez is only partially accepted, since truth is here intercepted by another delusion—that the British navy can bring about the economic ruin of Russia, even though debarred from the combative sphere of this war.

Though the international economic relationship has been entirely altered since the establishment of the British Empire, there still remains unchanged, as inflexible as it was in the beginning, the belief that the same factors still control the trade of the world, and that those factors, as potent as they are unchangeable, belong to the British Isles. To the same degree that this was true at one time it is untrue under modern conditions. When overland communication between continental states reached that degree of efficiency that their intercommunication in speed and capacity equaled or exceeded that by sea, continental nations become exempt from the economic domination held by insular powers through their command of the sea-routes of trade. Now the old conditions are, and in the future will be, reversed, and freedom from circumscription during war has passed to the continental states. Economic dependence and complete circumscription during war has become the lot of insular powers. Nowhere is this law of economic inviolability now conserved to continental states more clearly shown than in an attempted economic destruction of Russian trade by British control of the sea.

Approximately two-thirds of Russian imports and exports are by land frontiers, which makes this proportion immune from British naval power. Of the other one-third, or oceanic trade, more than ninety per cent. is carried by vessels other than Russian. Not one per cent. of Russian trade would be affected in time of war by British control of the sea, since only one-third of its trade is oceanic, and this is carried almost entirely by neutral vessels. Should it become necessary for Russian trade to abandon oceanic waterways, this one-third of her foreign trade would be passed to the sea through her neutral land frontiers, leaving the entire British navy to stare and wonder, helpless upon the seas.

When one nation contemplates the economic subjugation of another nation in the time of war, its determination must be governed by the character of the enemy's exports and imports. If the enemy's exports are principally manufactured goods, and its imports food-stuffs, then its economic subjugation is certain if the routes by which these food-stuffs are imported are seized. If, on the other hand, the nation has abundance of food and its imports are principally merchandise and manufactured articles, then its economic subjugation is impossible, even if all the routes by which this merchandise is carried are seized.

The character of the economic interrelationship between Russia and the British Empire betrays in itself the impossibility of British aspirations. So self-contained is Russia that ninety - seven and one-half per cent. of her exports are food-stuffs and raw material. Russian imports consist almost entirely of merchandise and manufactured articles, and of these imports fifty - seven per cent. are supplied by Germany. On the other hand, English imports consist almost entirely of food-stuffs and raw material, their exports consisting in the same degree of manufactured articles. Russian exports to the United Kingdom are food-stuffs and raw material; England's exports to Russia manufactured goods of the same class as those imported from Germany. For England, even if it were possible, to stop the oceanic trade of Russia, the result would be exactly opposite to that anticipated: it would close one source from which the United Kingdom derives its food and raw materials. It would destroy British export trade to Russia, and would increase that of Germany to Russia fifty per cent., since Great Britain does not supply Russia with a single article that is not at the present time supplied by Germany.

In a strategic sense we witness the inutility of the British navy to hinder or retard the Russian conquest of Asia, and in its economic phase we witness in this same war this strange paradox, that the utilization of the naval power of Great Britain to destroy the economic trade of Russia results disastrously only to the British Empire, while Russia remains economically as immune as though the British flag were not upon the seas.

The defense of India and those regions dependent upon it belongs wholly to the land forces of the Empire. Yet such is the strategic situation governing the attack and defense of India—the relative positions of the Russian and Saxon, as they cling to the northern and southern slopes of the Hindu-Kusch, together with their respective lines and bases—that the British army, as it now exists, could do no more than retard for a moment of time the progression of Russian conquest.

We have heretofore shown that there exists in the world certain places that have for mankind a strange and fatal significance, in that they give direction to his conquests. In these places victories are decisive, and defeats mark the consummation of national ruin. These places are the doorways through which nations come and go; sometimes arches of triumph; sometimes those narrow exits through which nations, like men, pass to return no more. Herat is one of these places; Kabul another. In all the world there are no two like them. Nowhere have highways resounded with the burden of greater armies or echoed with the triumph of greater conquerors. More than two thousand years ago it was said that he who possesses the key to Herat can unlock the door to India, and now, though these many centuries have passed, it remains as true as then.

The British lines are four hundred and sixty miles south of this city, while a Russian railroad station is eighty miles to the north. While only now and then a Saxon gazes furtively down upon its walls, there is never a time when watchers on its towers cannot discern to the northward, eastward, and westward the camp-fires of Cossack posts.

Russian advance upon India is by two ways: on the left flank by Afghanistan, and on the right flank by Persia.

The primary base of the Russian left advance is the Turkestan sphere.[1] This base of less than ten millions of people contains a Russian peace army of 135,000 men; its center at Samarkand is less distant from Herat than is Chicago from New York, while the primary base of the Russian right advance through Persia is the Caucasus sphere with a population of eleven million and a peace army of 125,000 men.

[1] Chart III.

The secondary bases of these two spheres are the Saratof sphere on the left, with a population of sixteen million and a peace army of 170,000 men, and the Kharakof sphere, with a population of forty-four million and a peace army of 450,000 men. These secondary spheres are common to both the right and left flanks, and are no greater distance from Herat than is New Orleans from New York.

From these four spheres [1] Russia is able to place in the field 880,000 men without affecting the military integrity of either her European or east Asian frontiers and under conditions entirely different from those controlling the Russo-Japanese conflict, where the theater of war was more than six thousand miles distant from these same spheres. Yet Russia was able to place in the field more than one million inhabitants.

The theater of war within which is determined the conquest of India is no longer vast, but, on the other hand, is governed by military distances such as affect the march of armies less great and less difficult than those that mark the conquests and triumphs of Napoleon. This theater of war is circumscribed within an area no greater than was the American Civil War. During the campaigns of that struggle the food and munitions of the Union armies were in many instances carried over a third greater distance than now intervenes between Russia and the strategic center of Indian conquest.

[1] Chart III.

The defense of India is governed by the application of two laws. Both are the product of conditions over which the Saxon has no control.

1. The defeat of Russia upon any of her frontiers other than that of India or Persia not only does not retard her advance upon India, but accelerates it.

2. The defense of the Indian frontiers is determined, not by British advice, but by the capacity and progression of Russian offense.

It must be a reaction instant in its application, proportionate in its intensity, and as continuous as the causes that gave to it its initial impulse.

V

SAXON STRUGGLE FOR SURVIVAL—GERMANY

Military Relationship of Germany and England.—Source and Cause of German Expansion.—Specific Preparation for War.—Results of Naval Engagements.—Theaters of War in Relation to Base.—Belgium, Holland, and Denmark.—British Policy toward Europe.—Principles Governing.

NATIONS are more often than otherwise given over to self-deception; but in no instance is the falsity of their deductions more pronounced than in their ideas concerning the mechanical means of war and the undue pre-eminence they give to them. Only when these means are restricted to one combatant do they affect the outcome of war. Inventions are generally regarded only in the wonder of their own mechanism, and not in their exact application to war. There is no differentiation made between their destructiveness and the possibility of using them at a time and place where they will affect, to the desired degree, the combative or resistant power of the enemy. In a sense, mechanical means of warfare are primarily the instruments of the offensive—man, the earth, and all natural forces constituting the defensive.

The making and invention of military appliances,

202

from the time when man in his old vast solitudes whittled out his first club until the creation of the last battle-ship, has been one long ceaseless labor to secure through artificial means the dominion of the offensive over the defensive; a struggle to give to the inanimate supremacy over the living forces of nature. This can never be. All weapons are limited in their application, and are designed to overcome not general but specific conditions. Man and nature alone constitute the universal and constant factors of war.

With every new military invention man is inspired with the belief that war is at an end. Yet each succeeding decade betrays the illusion of such futile hopes—the inutility of mechanics to end war or to exercise over it any effect beyond a limited and specific sphere.

It has been due to this abnormal belief that the British nation has exaggerated the power of its navy in extending its spheres of operations to regions it cannot reach, and the doing of deeds unknown in war. It has given to it a universality it does not possess. Its command over great nations has decreased with each successive decade, not so much through the application by other states of greater instruments of war as by means that have first to do with the affairs of peace.

Only when expansion of other nations converges upon and threatens the integrity of the British Empire by sea can its navy prevent the curtailment of its sovereignty or the dissolution of the Empire. When the destructive convergence of other nations is by land, as has just been shown in the expansion of Russia toward India, Persia, and eastern Asia, then the navy must give way to those means of war that belong to land.

The military relationship of Germany to the British Empire possesses a twofold significance. While the Saxon can deal with Russia only on land, or Japan only by sea, the conduct of a war with Germany includes both land and sea. The severity of this struggle will be equal to the means and forces employed: twice as great as against a continental state strategically placed, as Russia, or an insular power, as Japan.

Only in a war with an insular nation is the navy pre-eminent. In a war against Russia it has no place. In an offensive conflict with Germany it is of secondary importance. The British navy has one duty — to remain supreme in its sphere, the sea. From the beginning to the end it is restricted to the defensive. The army alone possesses the power capable of deciding the war and insuring such peace as will prolong the existence of the Empire.

As it is essential to the future greatness of Germany to destroy Saxon sovereignty and grow great upon its ruins, so it is the first duty of the British nation to arrest or destroy German power.

The failure of the British people to understand the principles that impel German aggression is only a repetition of that old error which nations make whenever they deal with conditions that involve themselves. When they attempt to differentiate between the immaterial and the immutable, the transient and the eternal, all that which is trivial and fleeting invariably takes precedence and controls their activities.

The British nation does not understand that German expansion is governed, not by the passions of her people, that vary from dawn to dusk; nor the ambitions of her ministers, that ebb and flow with the rise and decline of their parties; but by principles that have their origin in natural forces, and, in their impulse and propulsion, are not cognizant of time nor place, nor the hopes and fears, nor the valor or evasion, of mankind.

When the convergence of two races reaches the degree of acuteness now existing between the Saxon and the Teuton, it invariably results in war. There is no instance in history where the political relationship of two races, approximating that which now exists between the British and German Empires— where one exerts its utmost to prepare for war and the other, by evasion and subterfuge, seeks its postponement—did not result in one of those decisive wars which mark with fatal invariability the end of the unmartial race.

In the national misconception of war and the means that govern its conduct under varying conditions, the tendency of a nation is to throw itself upon the protection of the strongest means at its disposal, regardless of their utility or actual power, regardless of the conditions that direct and determine the combat, its purposes, or theater of war. So as races have done heretofore, under like conditions the British nation stakes its perpetuation upon its naval forces.

The British people conceal from themselves the true source and cause of German expansion. They regard it in the same light as they do their internal affairs. To them it is as transient as their passions, as mutable as their ideals. To them this coming together of the Teuton and the Saxon is political instead of racial.

It is in consequence of these two errors—the mistaken conception of the origin of the approaching struggle, its causes and effects, and the choice of the means with which to conduct war—that results in a third and determinate error assuring the defeat and dismemberment of the Saxon race. This error lies in the choice of the theater of war, and, though voluntarily chosen by the British people, it constitutes the last place where war should be waged or battles fought.

The purpose of an Anglo-Teutonic war is two-fold: that of Germany to destroy British sovereignty and create a Germanic world empire upon its ruins; that of England to defend its possessions, to arrest the militant expansion of the German race and limit its suzerainty over Europe. The task of

Germany is simple; that of England difficult. With the destruction of the British fleet, British capacity to wage war is at an end. England is invaded. This invasion is starvation. Before harvest there is only enough food in the United Kingdom to last for a few weeks; after the gathering of the crops only enough to last a few months.[1] But long before physical starvation sets in moral starvation will have accomplished its work.

The courage of a populace is at the best of times anemic. It ever has and ever will hover near the border-line of cowardice. So constant is it in cause and effect that we know with exactitude the manner and degree of its application.

The ease of German conquest over the British people is due to three factors:

1. The insular character of the Empire, which, in modern times, is the most precarious of all national existence.

2. The specific character of German preparation for war in a known and determinate theater, which gives a maximum of power to a minimum of effort and expense.

3. The decline of Saxon militancy; the abandonment of natural frontiers; the supremacy of individual wants over affairs of state; the disintegration of racial unity, and the evasion by the masses of their obligations to the Empire.

Owing to these conditions the task of Germany in

[1] Report of Royal Commission.

bringing about the dissolution of the British nation is relatively an easy one; that of the Saxon proportionately difficult, not only because of the reasons given, but due to military restrictions which should but do not control their preparation for war. We have said that if Germany gains control of the sea the war is brought to a close by this single act, and ends in the downfall of the Empire. On the other hand, should the British navy destroy that of Germany, the only result is that conditions remain the same as they were before the war, with this exception, that the United Kingdom is exempt from immediate disaster. But this victory brings England no nearer the destruction of German power and its potentialities for world expansion than prior to the war. Nothing except the ruin of the British navy increases German sovereignty in Europe more surely than the defeat of her own fleets.

The British, as well as the German, Empire possesses a definite purpose in this war so vital that its preparation should be carried on with the same vigor, the same intentness, that now characterizes the German. Unless the British Empire is able to take those military measures that will result in the destruction of German capacity to wage war, then its naval victories are useless.

To procrastinate against the inevitable is the culmination of human folly.

The degree of British military preparation, its character and objective, is simple, and requires no discussion, debate, nor hesitancy. The degree and purpose of German military power alone determine British military preparation. This is a state of preparedness that will not only assure victory over German armies, but control over the means out of which they are made and the potentialities that call them into being.

British military delinquency is not alone due to these factors just stated, but also arises from a misconception of a principle that governs the progress and consummation of war—the failure to differentiate between a theater of war and the base, to understand that what constitutes a decisive theater for one combatant is dangerous in a like degree to the other.

In this approaching struggle, as in all other wars, both nations have their choice of the theater of war, and it invariably follows that the selection of one is the danger of the other. It can be considered as a military maxim, true throughout all time and under all conditions, that, to the nation capable of determining the theater of war and maintaining it, the chances of success, as determined by historical precedent, stand in proportion of seven to three.

There is no single element that determines eventual victory or defeat with greater certainty than the relationship the theater of war bears to the combatants. Great victories gained in a wrongly chosen theater have little or no effect upon the final result, while minor victories gained at strategic points in the true theater of war possess the most definite character.

We have shown the relative value of a sea victory to Germany and to the British Empire—decisive on the part of Germany; without effect on the part of England. Because of this the true theater of war, from a German standpoint, is the sea; while the only decisive victories obtainable by the Saxon are from land battles fought on or adjacent to German soil. This is a cruel truism, but one that must remain so long as the hopes of the Empire are based alone upon its naval forces.

The elemental principles of warfare remain constant in their application, though the means of waging war vary with every age, every alteration of human association and advances made in science. Likewise the relative value of a base to the theater of war remains constant, their interdependability being still governed by the same principles as in former times. While the complexity of modern civilization has increased the value and vulnerability of a base it has also given equal importance to the theater of war through the increased decisiveness of a single battle. The result, therefore, of modern civilization has been the proportionate increase of the vulnerable character of the base and the decisive character of the theater of war. This equable development makes necessary a greater security and increased preparation for the defense of a base, and a corresponding ability to determine the theater of war.

The belief that the nearer the theater of war is to a base the greater its advantage must now be put aside, since it is true only so long as the means of transportation are limited. In war distance means, not miles, but time and capacity. Under modern conditions the greater the geographical distance the main base or nation is from the theater of war, the longer and with least hardship can it conduct the struggle, provided that the ratio of the maximum distance remains constant with a minimum capacity and rapidity of transportation as determined by the conditions of war.

Every advance in science increases the proximity of all bases and theaters; hence a corresponding increase in the geographical distance between a theater of war and base augments the endurance and defensive capacity of the nation, while the offensive ability is in no way restricted as long as its transportation facilities are provided for in accordance with the law just given.

Military operations can have only one true objective—the destruction of the enemy's capacity to wage war by seizing or destroying his armies, government, or resources. Hence, when the theater of war revolves around the main base, which is within the nation itself, the chances of defeat, all other military conditions being equal, are three and one-half times greater than when the theater of war is at a distance or in the enemy's territory.

In great and widely extended nations, as that of the British, there are many bases main to their specific spheres, but secondary as regards the empire. The United Kingdom differs from these secondary bases in that it is not only the base from which must be directed a European war, but is also the main base of the Empire.

Whenever the English nation is involved in war with a European power the interests of the entire Empire are affected. But when the United Kingdom is itself considered by the British people as the true theater of war in a conflict with a European state, and preparation for war made upon this principle, then the day of the Saxon is soon over and his Empire gone.

In a European war the surrounding seas, as well as the United Kingdom, constitute the Saxon base; [1] since, as we have shown, the boundaries of an insular nation are not its own coasts, but the exterior shores of the sea in which it is situated. The seas surrounding the British Islands are just as much a part of the British base as the Islands themselves. To prepare to carry on a European war in the United Kingdom or upon its seas is to commit as great an error as is to be found in military history. The British base reaches to the shores of Europe. The British theater of war only begins on those

[1] Chart IV.

coasts and extends eastward to that vital center which, if seized or destroyed, ends the war.

The relative position of the German base and choice of the theater of war is the reverse of the above. Were it not for the interposition of Belgium, the Netherlands, and Denmark, the coast-line of the North Sea would constitute a line of demarcation; eastward of which would be the German base and the Saxon theater of war; westward the English base and German theater.[1] The intervention of Belgium, the Netherlands, and Denmark along the line that limits these respective bases and theaters of war affects Germany and England only in the time of peace, when warfare is viewed in all that complexity which circumscribes the peaceful association of nations and belongs in no way to the brutal simplicity of war. The neutrality of these three states, whose boundaries are coincident with those lines of military demarcation that separate the German and Saxon races, results only in widening that line to the exact width of their territories.[2]

The neutrality of a minor state, once it is included in the theater of war waged between greater nations, becomes an anomaly. A kingdom in such a position invariably constitutes an area over which war is waged until one or the other combatant is capable of incorporating it within his base and forcing the conflict into the territories of the enemy. The neutralization of these three countries has increased,

[1] Chapter x, book i.   [2] Chart IV.

and not diminished, the probabilities of war. Only when they have been strategically incorporated within the base of the British Empire, their eastern and southern boundaries constituting its military frontiers in Europe, will it be possible for them or the Empire to endure.

British policy toward Europe is governed by three principles, the simplicity of which permits no erroneous deductions and their directness no evasion:

1. Whenever a European nation acquires, through war or material development, that degree of potential strength and actual military force that it controls the power of Europe, it will in due time direct the totality of this power toward the destruction of the British Empire.

2. Whenever it becomes apparent that one European state or racial coalition is seeking the overlordship of Europe in the manner above stated, it at once becomes imperative upon the British nation to destroy this power and the means that make it possible.

3. The British Empire can only subject Europe to her will by the control of two strategic spheres:

> (a) The mastery of the Mediterranean, within which as affecting the British Empire is included part of Russia, the Turkish Empire, Austria-Hungary, Italy, and a part of France and Spain. This theater of war belongs to the British navy, the strength of its fleets being

determined by the maximum strength of any coalition that may be brought against it.

(*b*) The northern strategic sphere includes military control over Denmark, the Netherlands, and Belgium. British military occupation of Denmark, in the event of war, restricts Russia to the land, and forbids her the sea, limiting that great power to only one avenue of attack upon the Empire—that of the Indian frontier. This position, moreover, annuls the strategic value of the Kiel Canal by making the Baltic an inland sea. With the military occupation of Belgium and the Netherlands German aggression by sea is restricted to the mouth of the Elbe, a strategic circumscription which makes impossible Teutonic expansion seaward. German naval supremacy must first be based on the command of the North Sea, which alone is determined by the military control of Denmark, and only in a secondary degree by the command of the mouths of the Rhine and the Scheldt.

4. Political policies not directed toward the defense of these two strategic spheres are erroneous, and military preparation governed by any other principle than that based upon actual military control will prove useless.

VI

PREPARATION AND CONFLICT

Military Preparation and National Survival.—No Line of Demarcation Between Peace and War.—Insecurity of British Empire in Relation to Germany.—Necessary to Assume Offensive.—Neutrality of Small Nations.—Principles Governing Wars Involving Neutral States.

IN modern times, when war ensues between nations whose military preparedness approaches the maximum of their capacity and states whose military preparation is reduced to a minimum, the progress and consummation of war is ascertainable before armies take the field. Subsequent conflicts have little or no place in its determination; they no more than mark with their tragic milestones the old red way along which neglectful nations hasten to their end.

The degree of continuity and the character of preparation for war constitute the determinate principle in its progression toward victory or defeat. Only between nations whose preparations during peace are relatively equal does the subsequent period of conflict constitute a decisive factor. It is no longer possible to trust to the fortunes of war, for these, like its gods, have abandoned mankind.

Even genius falters in this new mechanic age, and valor and pride, for no longer can these things, noble and heroic as they are, be substituted for a lack of preparation in one state nor overcome it in another.

Military provision in modern times has come to bear so intimate a relationship to national survival that it forms the principle upon which must be based such laws as direct its progress and prolong its existence. Preparation for war is no longer an orderless gathering together of tribes or levies or militia or volunteers; neither the building of arsenals nor the cramming of them with the utensils of combat. These old ideals have no more than a subordinate place in that general adjustment made necessary by this age, and upon the completeness of which depends the duration of national life.

The error of Saxon preparation for war originates in Saxon misconception of peace. Peace and war are but relative terms descriptive of human struggle as divided into two phases. Absolute peace between nations only exists prior to the time their association begins. When the intercourse between individuals of one nation and those of another increases to the point that their trade becomes competitive, it involves the interests that control the policies of state. The transition from the material conflict of individual acquisitiveness to the combative struggle of national wants is as imperceptible in its progression as is that growth which marks the gradual transition from individual greed to national necessity.

There is no line of demarcation between peace and war. In all the struggles of the human race we are unable to determine with exactitude the beginning of a single war. The difference between war and peace is not that which distinguishes quietude from conflict. It is a difference only in manner and degree. It is but the temporary ascendancy of composite struggle over individual strife.

International war has no beginning and no end, so long as mankind brings himself together in political and individual contention. Whether it is for good or for evil, this everlasting struggle forms the necessary *motif* of human aspiration. Between a spider slipping his web from twig to leaf and a man threading his nets from threshold to threshold, between a nest of ants by the roadside and a tribe of men upon a greater way, there is no difference.

Individual strife is the epitome of selfishness; war a gigantic altruism.

Nations as individuals exist always in a state of potential combat. The degree of combative potentiality merges unperceived from the passive, which we call peace, to the active, which is known as war. War exists long before the public consciousness is aware of it, since nations, especially those in a low state of militancy, conceal from themselves as long as possible this transition. The dead may be upon the field before they acknowledge it, yet they have in reality been at war for an indefinite period of time.

A battle is not entirely fought on the day it is fought, nor the ensuing victory or defeat wholly due to the efforts of that day. A war with its campaigns and battles bears the same relation to the preceding peace that a battle does to the period of war that preceded it. A battle is a part of war; war a part of peace. We cannot determine where one ends and the other begins. A battle is but a moment of violent human activity, and is the result of innumerable other conditions and activities that have preceded it in regular sequence. So a war is only a battle prolonged in time and space. A battle in its relationship to war is analogous to war in its relationship to peace. In a battle, those factors that determine the success or failure belong to the combat only in a limited sense. Months of war may precede the battle, yet toward and for that battle the nations have been constantly preparing for every contingency. This attitude of a nation toward preparation for a battle during the months of war that precede it must, in a greater sense, be the same toward war during the years of peace that go before it. To deny preparation for war during peace is a greater folly than to refuse to prepare for battle after war has begun.

Formerly preparation for war was not only limited to a small portion of the population, but, being simple in character and applied to a people

more or less inured to conflict, it neither required
a long period of time nor great effort on the part of
the nation. In modern times, however, preparation
for war and war itself affect the entire state. Every
part of society, every business, every profession now
has a definite place in relation to war.

Before a state can be drilled to arms its spirit
must be militant; if not, it must undergo such a
transfiguration. Militancy is different from other
virtues in that it cannot be preserved by the individual. It is collective, and not personal; hence the
first duty devolving upon a state is to take means
of preserving from deterioration this excellence
upon which depends its existence. Modern life has
a definite effect upon the militant decadence of a
race, in that it diminishes in proportion as the complexity of civilization is increased. So positive is
the result of this deterioration that those nations
not having compulsory training are incapable of
entering into war with a power whose preparation
is inclusive of enforced military service.

It has been shown that those factors upon which
the security of the British nation depends, and the
theaters of war where battles must be fought, are
without the confines of the Empire. Once these
frontiers are forced the defense of the Empire is at
an end. Because of this, British military preparation, the organization and character of its forces,
can never be governed by the principle of defending
the Empire within its own segregated territories.

In an empire so constituted as that of the British, an army of home defense becomes an army of imperial destruction.

A foreign army on English soil and England becomes the sepulcher of the Saxon race.

British military preparation and the organization of every unit constituting its military force, whether in the United Kingdom, Australia, Canada, South Africa, or its colonies, must be subject to and governed by those principles that determine the character of an expeditionary force.

As the defense of Australia belongs primarily to the defense of the Indian frontiers, so Australia constitutes a base from which, to the Indian theater of war, forces must be sent. Canada, South Africa, and the colonies depend upon the hegemony of the United Kingdom. Its survival is in turn dependent upon the defense of the frontiers of Belgium, the Netherlands, and Denmark. In the European theater of war the United Kingdom forms the main base, while the dependent dominions and colonies constitute secondary bases from which to the common theater of war troops must be despatched.

British military preparation necessitates not only harmony of action, but cohesiveness of effort and a singleness of purpose as wide as the world itself. It necessitates not alone vast means of transportation, but a constant increase in their efficiency, so that their rapidity and capacity shall maintain the preliminary theater of war at no greater distance from

British bases than from those of the enemy. The most complete military preparedness is useless if it cannot be utilized at a crucial time or in the true theater of war.

These salient needs are ordinarily controlled by civil authorities who are not conscious of what makes military strength. They invariably neglect moments of greatest military value, and are seldom cognizant of the true theater of war. This ignorance increases as military control over the departments of state diminishes. This reconstruction of governmental ideals constitutes the basis of all future preparation for war as it affects the duration and futurity of the Saxon race.

The growth of the Saxon Empire and the development of its power have not been due so much to Saxon statesmanship as to the lack of it in those states whose territories now form its domains. Whenever the intelligence and activity of Saxon statesmen becomes less than that exercised by its strongest opponent, or, remaining stationary in international progression, is superceded, then it must share the fate of those nations whose sovereignty it destroyed to secure the power now so vast in potentiality and so useless in its own preservation.

Nations, like individuals, seldom profit when they succeed through the ignorance of others and take no measures to prevent the success of others through their own ignorance.

Saxon power, potential and actual, is in a state

of erosion—a condition due not so much to the superior intelligence of those nations whose forces and persistence now grind and wear away its sides, as to its own failure to realize that for a nation to stand still in universal progression is identical, in its results, with retrocession—a reversion on the part of a state to an earlier phase of international relationship, the value of which has passed away forever.

Power and progress are no more than relative terms. The increasing inequality of German and British power is due not so much to the superiority of German progress as to the stationary character of British development, not so much to German intelligence as to Saxon indifference. That which constitutes the basic element of German military power, as exercised against the British Empire, results from British ignorance, instead of German wisdom, in all matters appertaining to warfare, and a consequent violation on part of British statesmen of three principles of war:

1. Permitting the continuance of false military ideals and preparation no longer suitable to modern conditions of war.

2. Selecting a false theater of war and including the base of the Empire within this theater.

3. By the sum of these errors restricting the initiation of war to the enemy.

So long, therefore, as statesmen violate these principles with the sanction and applause of the populace, all other military preparation is useless. Armies and navies, heroism and suffering, are of no avail in this old immolation of the nation by the ignorance of its people—in this old hecatomb of its vanity, in this last feeble sacrifice of its valor.

Whenever it is determined, as it can be with exactitude, that the convergence of international interests is acute, general preparation for war must become specific. When the rate of speed by which nations move to the point of contact has been ascertained, it devolves upon the ministers of state to anticipate any overt act on the part of the enemy and initiate the war.

When a state does not initiate war it commits its first error against the principle of military science. When it waits to make ready for war after hostilities have been declared, it only prepares to destroy itself.

So essential is this principle of initiation to success in warfare that within the last two hundred years there is no instance where sufficient warning has been given that permitted the enemy to undertake military preparation. The necessity of a declaration of war is only a modern illusion. During the last two centuries we have less than ten cases where declarations have been issued prior to the regular commencement of hostilities, though in one form or another war already existed. During this same period of time we have one hundred and eleven cases where war was begun without any notification.

PREPARATION AND CONFLICT

No nation has followed more persistently than the English this principle of making war without prior declaration. They have done so, as have others, because the initiation of a conflict constitutes the most essential principle of warfare.

Formerly armies reached the theater of war by degrees, owing to the great distance that separated states and the poverty of means of communication. A march of armies from one state to another was slow, cumbersome, and incapable of surprise. It was in itself a notification of war made in sufficient time for nations, in their primitive fashion, to prepare; hence a formal notification influenced neither in one way nor the other the activities of war. In modern times, however, means of transportation and communication have been so developed by science that the old natural barriers have been broken down. In the future it can be considered as an established principle that nations will more and more make war without previous notification, since modern facilities increase their ability to take their opponents by surprise and to strike the first blow as nearly as possible to their main base. That this is true is shown by the fact that the number of wars undertaken without any prior declaration of hostilities in the nineteenth century is greater than in the eighteenth. During the former century there are recorded forty-seven wars begun without any prior declaration, while in the nineteenth eighty wars were begun without any prior declaration. So correct is this principle governing the initiation of future wars that Saxon preparation for war must be based upon it. Whenever the inevitability of a conflict is recognized, as is the case with both Germany and Russia, where the theaters of war are remote from their bases, they should proceed to specific preparation for the conflict, and, when they reach the maximum of preparation, initiate the war by the occupation of those frontiers upon which depends the destiny of the Empire.

The occupation of the Persian and Afghanistan frontiers prior to war with Russia, or the European frontiers in a conflict with Germany, arouses in the British nation the appearance of great opposition to the violation of neutral territory. This is false, for the Empire is not moved by the sanctity of neutrality. It is only a means of evading responsibility and shifting it upon these nations, deluding themselves with the belief that such declarations are inviolable; whereas, no nation has violated neutral territory and denied their obligations more frequently than the Saxon. But, now that Saxon sovereignty depends upon the defense of these frontiers, we see the British race laying itself open to destruction under the delusion that that which has no real existence will defend them.

The occupation by the Saxon of these frontiers is a territorial and not a moral violation, while their occupation by Russia, on the one hand, and Germany, on the other, only precedes the final passage of their identity, that tragic end under the swirl and spawning of these two races.

Neutrality of states under the conditions just mentioned has never heretofore nor will in future have any place in international association in time of war. Such neutrality is a modern delusion. It is an excrescence.

In the year 1801 the island of Madeira was taken possession of by the British, without any previous communication to the Court of Lisbon, in order that it should not fall into the hands of the French, observing in this action the true principle governing such activities in war.

In 1807 the British fleet, without any notification, with no intimation given of hostile intentions, no complaint of misconduct on the part of Denmark, entered the Baltic, seized the Danish fleet, and blockaded the island of Zealand, on which is situated the city of Copenhagen. At this time both nations had their ambassadors residing in their respective capitals and were in perfect harmony. The purpose of this attack was to anticipate the occupation of Denmark and the use of her fleets by France. So correct is the principle of this initiation that it stands out with remarkable brilliancy in the darkness of innumerable military errors made by the Saxon race.

If England were, therefore, justified in seizing Denmark in the beginning of the nineteenth century for no other reason than to prevent the employ-

ment of the Danish fleet by the French, how much
more is she justified during peace in the twentieth
century in the occupation of its southern frontiers
for the protection of both nations against German
aggression.

That this principle was applicable in the beginning
of the nineteenth century, but is not so under the
civilization of the twentieth, is an erroneous conception of the principles that direct the conflict of
nations. While England and other nations violated
both peace and neutrality in the beginning of the
nineteenth century, we find Russia and Japan doing
the same thing in China and Korea in the beginning
of the twentieth.

These old laws are not cognizant of man nor those
ordinances by which he would rope down the immutable with the gauzy threads he spins in that
moment of sunlight that marks his wisdom and his
flight.

Wars involving neutral states are governed by
three principles:

1. Whenever a minor state rests between the bases
of two combatants and constitutes a portion of the
subsequent theater of war, it is essential to seize
that state prior to or at the beginning of a war,
either for one's own advantage or to prevent it from
falling into the hands of the enemy.

2. When the neutrality of a minor state constitutes an element of weakness to a great power, those
frontiers from which arise the weakness should al-

ways be subject to the control of the military
power.

3. When the continental neutrality or independence of a minor state threatens the existence of a
great power, as Korea threatened Japan, it should
be deprived of its independence and absorbed by
the greater power.

VII

UNITY OF FORCES

Principles Governing the Unity of Empire.—Political and Military
Power Must Remain in Hands of a Racial Unit.—Sectional Distinctions Must be Destroyed.—Confederacy of Independent
States the Weakest Form of Government.—Military Consolidation Necessary to Preservation of Empire.

WE now pass to the end of our work. There
has been much that is bitter in what we have
written and the inevitability of our conclusions. It
could not be otherwise. We have shunned hope and
its illusions, theory and its pitfalls, evasion and its
massacres. We have been guided, not by those
transient ideals that ordinarily direct human aspiration, but by that truth that is found in the orderly
sequence of natural laws, in their immutability and
the finality of their application.

Whatever, if any, superiority exists in the Saxon
race has nothing to do with the prolongation of
national life, unless its superior intelligence acts in
accordance with these laws and is cognizant at all
times of the ephemeral character of national and
racial existence in contrast to the inexorability of
those eternal forces that control the progression
and dissolution of political entities.

The survival of the British Empire depends upon a differentiation between national greatness and national power. When the government of an empire is the product of sectional policies that endure no longer than the men who make them and rise no higher than the mediocrity of public impulse, they are not the synthesis of national intelligence, but that stronger synthesis of individual ignorance and selfishness as expressed in the wild, mad laws of mob caprice.

The perpetuation of the British Empire depends, first, upon its military unity, and, secondly, upon its political unification. Sectionalism in time and place must give way to laws so universal in their application that they differentiate in no way between the inhabitants of the oversea dominions and the United Kingdom.

The unity of the Empire cannot be a sentimental union of its component parts, neither can it be a confederacy of independent political units. The first is a negative cause of disintegration, the second a positive one. This unification is governed by four principles:

1. The Empire must be militarily a unit.

2. It must be politically as cohesive as a single state.

3. The military and political supremacy of the Saxon in its constituent parts.

4. The complete subordination of the Empire to the unity of the whole.

As an individual does not understand the true relation existing between himself and the state, exaggerating the immaterial and denying the essential, so do segregated portions of a nation fail to view in their true light the universal activities of national existence, but, on the other hand, seek to circumvent national power by the intrusion of their own desires. When this is true in an empire scattered over the world as that of the Saxon, it involves such a nation in constantly increasing dangers, for the liability of war is almost invariably in proportion to the number of parts into which maritime nations are divided and possess a potential value to others.

As the Empire has added to its possessions it has augmented the number of its enemies. There is now no political sphere in the world where the interests of one or more nations are not directed against those of the Saxon and are convergent to the degree that the end in each instance is war.

While the Saxon Empire has increased in greatness, it has lost in power through three reasons:

1. Failure to add to its power in constant ratio to its increase in greatness.

2. Failure to augment its power relative to the increase of power among those nations whose interests have or will become convergent.

3. Failure to realize the change modern means of transportation and communication have brought about in international association, shrinking the

world, jamming nations one against the other, increasing contention, and turning the whole vast world with all its once sequestered places into a single theater of war.

National exertion for defense must be made in proportion to the probabilities of war. Who then is there that can limit the labors of the Saxon Empire, from whose dominions even the sun cannot escape, and because of whose sovereignty no nation can move? Yet the Saxon race has never grasped the conception involved in the majesty of an endless Empire and in the solemn grandeur of its perpetuation.

The tendency of human society is not, as is generally believed, toward unity, but is actuated by disintegrating influences which are the result of the magnification of their own personalities or localities. Mankind through past ages has continued to assemble together in larger and larger units due to the necessity of self-protection. Whenever there occurs a lull in international progression so that mutual protection among racial or geographical constituencies is no longer a necessity, there results that sectional and racial ascendancy which ends in dissolution.

National disintegration originates in peace, and is the result of the dissolution of political and racial unity.

When a nation made up of autonomous parts possesses no restrictive unifying elements, it is lacking in solidarity to the degree that the autonomy of its component parts is complete.

Some nations are politically homogeneous and racially heterogeneous. The unity of such a state is greater than if the reverse of these conditions were true. A nation politically and racially homogeneous constitutes a unified state in its strongest and most natural form. A nation that is not only politically heterogeneous and racially heterogeneous, but also geographically devoid of any unity, constitutes the weakest form of empire, and necessitates the exercise of the greatest wisdom, of national fortitude and constancy, to counteract these natural elements of disintegration and dissolution.

The British Empire is a nation of this latter kind.

The British nation, thrown indifferently over the world, includes one-third of the human race, and of these less than one-seventh are Saxon. Upon this minority is fixed the responsibility of rule. For this privilege of dominion the Saxon must assume the full responsibility of Imperial defense. In a racially heterogeneous state the military and political power must remain in the hands of a single and homogeneous race. Whenever the dominant race shares his political and military power, the decadence of Imperial unity and durability begins.

So long as the political and military power remains in the hands of a single racial element the Empire will endure, provided that their power is superior to conditions of internal disintegration and the external erosive forces of convergent nations. But if the nation is a confederation of political units autonomous to the degree of the British dominions and, like them, geographically separate, the nation is exposed to the quickest and surest elements of political decadence and the absorption of its component parts when any one or more nations become stronger than its strongest units.

The effect of political autonomy upon the people of segregated portions of a state is distinct in character, though relative in the degree of influence it exercises over conditions that tend toward disintegration. Patriotism as ordinarily understood is not handed down from the heavens, but is, on the other hand, the product of earth. It is an attachment that mankind gathers only from the soil he tills. Yet it is this patriotism of environment, this old fealty of man for his tent-pegs and herds, that is in this age not only without utility, but becomes the foci of political disintegration.

Primitive patriotism is local, and to be of use in this age must, like the evolution of a race, pass through a corresponding transmutation. The small patriotism of environment must now be put aside forever. This is not a crucifixion of old ideals; it is a transfiguration. It is the merging of localities into universality. It is turning the eyes of an empire from the hopeless, stunted herbage at their feet to the constellations overhead, where once not many centuries ago some shepherds raised their narrowed eyes and found a universe.

The creation of an empire in a permanent sense is possible only subsequent to the destruction of all sectional distinctions. Whenever political autonomy exists to the degree that it makes possible sectional distinctions and gives to these localities political precedence over Imperial policies, unity is at an end and political disintegration begins.

In proportion as political autonomy is increased in a distant and segregated portion of the Empire, there is increased the localization of patriotism and all the evils that ensue from it. Whenever political autonomy is augmented to the degree that it clashes with Imperial ordinances, sectional rights invariably take precedence. This results in another form of political dissolution. The first effect will be a lack of political unity and a diffusion of patriotism throughout the Empire. This will sputter and go off like scattered grains of powder, giving forth possibly much smoke and some noise, but does no more than increase the probabilities of Imperial destruction.

The decrease of Imperial patriotism in segregated portions of the Empire is determinable by time. The fealty of a colony to the mother-country decreases in inverse ratio as is increased its self-government. Each generation leaves behind it local traditions; succeeding generations become more and more fixed to the soil that nourishes them.

Abstract ideals involving Imperial patriotism give way to that which is material and local. So strong is the supremacy of locality and its diurnal tasks over man, that conditions which are distant in time and space or ideals that are abstract have very little effect upon him. Nothing is more difficult than to raise the eyelids of man. He loves his own dirt, and glories in the fact that God made him out of it.

The preservation of Saxon racial integrity, together with their possessions and aspirations, depends primarily on a delocalization of their patriotism, the replacing of it by that other racial fealty which knows no geographical distinctions, and one that, instead of creeping along with the nose to the narrow spoor of old hates, is cognizant only of the race and Empire as a whole.

The demand for political autonomy is only justifiable when local independence does not interfere with the unity and solidarity of the Empire. Whenever the relationship between the different portions of the Empire takes the form of a confederacy in which the dominions or colonies assume such a degree of independence that they take upon themselves the prerogatives of their own defense and the right of determining whether or not they will assist in the defense of the other parts, then they destroy not alone themselves, but the Empire.

The ratio of population growth in these dominions is comparative to a like growth of the nations within whose sphere of expansion they happen to be. In consequence of this their military potentiality must remain, in its growth, at a relative fixed degree of inferiority. The economic growth of European and Asiatic nations, together with their demands for the unexploited resources of these dominions, increases in geometrical ratio, while the defensive capacity of the dominions, relative to these nations, either remains constant or depreciates. An independent Australia, regardless of its own efforts, can never withstand Japan, since the disproportion of their initial power is so great that in time Australia will become relatively weaker and Japan stronger. This is true of India in relation to Russia, Canada to the United States, Africa to Europe, and the United Kingdom to the Teutonic race.

Military unity constitutes the basis of national survival in an empire composed of politically autonomous states. A confederation of states in the form of an empire is significant of political instability. The error of British Imperial policy is this tendency toward a confederated form of government, giving to the constituent units not alone self-government, but military segregation.

Whenever the power of the self-governing colonies becomes inclusive of the military and naval prerogatives and constitutional rights for determining their use, such a nation will prove to be no more than a shell of mended pieces.

When a nation is composed of self-governing

states, each incapable of self-defense, their protection is to be found only in the unification of their military potentiality and its complete centralization. Military function adheres to a government only in its most unified form, so that to give to any portion of a state military independence, though it is politically autonomous, is to expose the entire Empire to destruction from external forces or dissolution through internal dissension.

Saxon greatness is only within itself, and constitutes no more than a single link in that endless chain of races that has wrapped itself around this world from a time that has for us no beginning to a time that likewise has no end.

If the Saxon race is to survive, it can do so only as a whole (1) through the military and naval unification of the Empire; (2) the complete separation of the military and naval systems from the civil government of the dominions and colonies; (3) the introduction of universal and compulsory military service among the Saxons throughout the Empire; (4) all armies to be organized on the basis of expeditionary forces; (5) the size and distribution of the Imperial armies to be determined by the size and distribution of its probable adversaries; (6) the militancy of the Saxon race, and the actual military power of the Empire increased with every military increment made by nations whose natural lines of expansion are toward territories and peoples now under British dominion; (7) the military and political unity of the Empire must progress toward greater centralization as the population of its component parts is increased.

In the contact of war, either offensive or defensive, a confederated form of government is the weakest. While the Saxon is more capable of self-government than many other races holding sovereignty over themselves or imposing it upon others, their capacity has not reached such a height that they are able to deny those elemental forces that take no cognizance of their limited superiority.

The Saxon has tried a confederacy of states, militarily as well as politically autonomous, and has found it to be wanting. In the formation of the American Republic, in the struggles and vicissitudes that have marked its progress from the beginning until the present time, is betrayed the inherent weakness of such a form of government and the impossibility of its survival. Had the American Republic, in the beginning of its independence, been subject to the same dangers to which every nation is now exposed through the intimacy of their intercourse and the shortness of the distance that intervenes between them, the Republic would not have survived a single generation. Yet, as we examine the progress which marks the evolution of its political system, we find that almost in exact proportion as science has brought it into closer contact with the rest of the world, augmenting its responsibilities and dangers, it has altered its political system, taking away the sovereign rights of the states; now silently, now with turmoil and noise, sometimes in convention halls, and sometimes upon fields of battle, the struggle to survive forced the American Republic to abandon a confederated form of government.

A confederacy is an old ignorance. It is a falsification of political independence, and has no more a place in a modern state than have those other blind errors nations have put away forever.

INDEX

ADELAIDE, 78–79.

Aden, 64.

Afghan, 109.

Afghanistan, 46, 199, 226.

Africa, 62, 67, 120, 182, 194, 238.

Alexander the Great, 42, 102.

America, unpreparedness for war, 7; relation to British Empire, 28–30; emigration to Canada, 31–33; racial expansion in, 39–40; possibility of war with Japan, 92; Civil War of, 200, 240–241.

Amur, 109.

Anglo-Japanese alliance, 87–91, 96.

Anglo-Saxon race, 8–9, 35–36.

Arabia, 63.

Arbela, battle of, 103, 171.

Asia, 16, 28, 47, 68, 70–71, 74, 87–88, 91–92, 97, 99, 104–105, 120–122, 126–127, 144, 157–158, 175, 182, 194–195, 204.

Asia Minor, 57, 63—64, 67, 115, 120, 146, 151, 190, 195.

Atlantic Ocean, 40, 90–91, 126, 175–176.

Austerlitz, battle of, 112, 121.

Australasia, immigration to, 35; defense of, is defense of India, 69; relation to Asian races, 70–71; home defense inadequate, 72–76; permanent defense naval, 77; strategic spheres of, 79; nature of defense, 81; value to Empire, 83; mutual obligations of Australia and Empire, 84; failure in duty to Imperial unity, 89; possible conquest by Japan, 93; defense can only be accomplished by Empire, 95; as effected by a German expansion in Pacific, 144.

Australia, 56; position in relation to India, 64, 67; blind to changing international conditions, 69; military spheres of, 78; restriction of population to sea-coasts, 79–80; defense divisible into two parts, 81; dependence upon Imperial solidarity, 82; relation to Indian defense, 221; could not resist Japan unaided, 238.

Austria, 75, 115, 123–124, 137, 140, 141, 146, 214.

BALKANS, 46, 115, 117, 122.

Baltic, 107–108, 110, 215, 227.

Batoum, 109.

Belgium, 46, 137, 160–161, 213, 215, 221.

Berlin, 135.

Bessarabia, 109.

Bismarck, Prince, 132, 133, 135.

Black Sea, 107–110, 120.

Blue Mountains, Australia, 80.

Boors, 81.

Bosphorus, 112, 114, 115, 118, 146.

Bredo, Peace of, 11.

Brisbane, 78, 80.

British Empire, 2; dangers to, 3–5; unpreparedness for war, 7; military system too fixed,

9–10; formation of, 11–12; laws governing future hostilities of, 13; dangers in its geographical distribution, 15–17; militant spirit weakened, 17–18; principles determining future wars against, 20–24; angles of convergence with other powers, 28; relationship toward America, 30; relations with Canada, 33–34; relationship with Western hemisphere, 36–39; security in Western hemisphere dependent on European equilibrium, 41; vastness of, no guarantee of duration, 42; spread of, due to strategic position of British Isles, 46; interposes between Europe and Asia, 47; importance of India to, 48, 66–67; development of India by, 49–51; duty to provide for India's expansion, 56; defense of frontiers, 60–62; relation to Pacific dominions, 68–69; absorption of Transvaal, 73; relation to Australasia, 74, 83–84; continental attributes of, 76; results of alliance with Japan, 87–90, 93; duty to restore equilibrium in Pacific, 94; alliance with China more advantageous than with Japan, 95–98; threatened in Asia by Russian advance, 105; ignorant of India's value to Empire, 113; *Dreibund* negative menace to, 123–124; expansion of other powers directed against dominions of, 125–128; law of expansion of, 131; relation to German expansion, 132–139; duration dependent upon balance of European power, 140–142; navy compared with Germany's, 145; vulnerable as are all empires, 149–152; zenith of power after Waterloo, 153–

155; retrocession of power in Asia, 157; end of political dominion over Europe, 158; preservation of Belgium, Holland, and Denmark necessary to, 160–161; causes of its dangers, 162–163; destruction of fleet means downfall of, 172; suzerainty of diminished, 173–175; naval force inadequate, 176–177; threatened by growth of other sea powers, 180; destruction of supremacy begins during peace, 183–185; failure to stop extension of convergent states, 187–191; national mind not militant, 192–193; navy powerless to prevent Russia's Asian expansion, 194; sea power powerless to destroy Russian trade, 195–198; distance of frontiers from Herat compared with those of Russia, 199; laws governing defense of India, 201; exaggeration of navy's value, 203; military relationship with Germany, 204–206; result of destruction of fleet, 207–208; importance in choice of theater of war, 209–212; principles governing policy toward Europe, 214–215; factors on which security depends, 220; necessity of offensive policy, 221; governmental ideals should be reconstructed, 222; violation by statesmen of principles of war, 223; wars begun without previous declaration, 225; opposition to violation of neutral territory, 226; blockade of Denmark, 227–228; principles governing unity of, 231; reasons for loss of power, 232–235; sectional distinctiveness must be destroyed, 236–237; weakness of confederated government from military standpoint,

INDEX

238; military consolidation necessary, 239–240.

British Islands, 32–33, 35, 46–47, 63, 143, 174, 212.

British statesmen, 19, 29, 34, 223.

Bug, 108.

Burma, 57, 67, 120.

Cæsar, Julius, 26.

Canada, nationalism of, 30; population, 31–34; immigration to, 35, 40; Indian subjects prohibited from domicile in, 56; less important to Empire than India, 69; American expansion against unsuccessful, 130; depends on hegemony of United Kingdom, 221; relation to United States, 238.

Cape Town, 64, 77.

Caribbean Sea, 145.

Carthage, 180.

Caspian Sea, 107, 109.

Caucasus, 107, 109, 120, 199.

China, military unpreparedness of, 7; Great Wall of, 16–17; decline of, 46; as continental state, 75; vastness of obscured growth of Japan, 85; Russian advance in, 89, 91; interests in common with India, 95; expansion antagonistic to Russia, 96–99; neutrality violated by Russia, 228.

China-Japanese War, 116.

Copenhagen, 227.

Crimea, 108.

Cyprus, 67.

Danube, 109.

Denmark, dangerous position of, 46; strategic importance to Germany, 137, 141–146; failure of England to preserve integrity of, 158; loss of provinces, 160–161; limits British and German bases of war, 213; necessity of military control of

to England, 215; occupation of by England, 227.

Diego Garcia, 64.

Disintegration, national, 2.

Dniester, 108.

Dreibund, interpolitical relationship of Russia, Japan, and Germany, 122–128.

Duration of empires, principle of, 42.

Dutch, possessions in America, 145–146; possessions in East Indies, decline of, 174.

Egypt, 46, 67.

Elbe, 215.

England, growth as maritime nation, 11–12; guarantees independence of American nations, 40, 47; invasion of, preferable to loss of India, 48; ignorance of India's value, 60; insular position of, 75; result of concentration against France and Russia, 85; position as effected by Japan's rise to power, 88; relation to Europe, 91–92; not naturally ally of Japan, 97; possible invasion by Germany, 105; results of failure to prevent German unity, 139–140; proximity to Holland, 143; supreme at close of Napoleonic wars, 153; danger to from lack of military expansion, 158; failure to realize Denmark's position, 160–161; strategic position of, 174; trade of, 197; results of an invasion of, 206–208, 221; bases in war, 213; violations of neutrality by, 227–228.

Euphrates, 115.

Eurasia, 119.

Europe, 28; emigration from, 32–33, 35; interests in America, 38–40; overflow to other continents, 47; difference between Europe and India, 50;

aggression against India, 64–65; size compared with Australasia's, 70; interests in Asia, 87–88, 105; wars of, 103; Russian aggression in, 112, 117–118, 120; Napoleon and, 135; balance of power in, 140; Denmark's position in, 142; relation to Monroe Doctrine, 146; expansion as influenced by modern science, 151; amalgamation of minor states in, 158; racial consolidation of, 159; in sixteenth century, 173–174; relation to British sea power, 175–177; intercommunication by land, 182; German power in, 188; movement on other continents, 194; Russian frontiers in, 200; British policy toward, 212, 215.

Expansion of races, 56–65.

FINLAND, 108.
Five Seas, 15.
Formosa, 93.
France, 11; decline of maritime power, 12; insular characteristics of, 75; English concentration against, 85; unaffected by Asia's awakening, 105; Napoleon's influence on expansion of, 132; relation to Germany, 136; native population of, 144; condition at close of Napoleonic wars, 153; decline of, 174; in Mediterranean, 214; designs on Denmark, 227.
Franco-Prussian War, 141.
French population in Canada, 31.
French Revolution, 12.
Friedland, 112.

GENGHIS KHAN, 42–43, 102.
Genoa, 11.
Germany, size and population compared with India's, 48; territorial expansion in relation to India, 59–60; eastern advance should be limited by England, 65; problems of defense, 75; menace to British Empire, 85; comparison of military forces with Japan's, 90; conquest feared by British, 105; rise and ambitions of, 112; relations to Russia, 115, 118, 121; natural ally of Russia and Japan against England, 122 – 124; results from possible wars, 125–126; dangers to British Empire in expansion of, 127–128; basic impulse of expansion, 131; influence of Bismarck, 132; development of power not a recent one, 133; zenith of militancy, 134; struggle with British Empire inevitable, 135–137, 138–140; strategic importance of Denmark to, 141–143, 215; laws governing naval expansion of, 144–145; expansion over Austria, 146; Waterloo beginning of military greatness of, 153; expansion as it affects Great Britain, 159–170; result of destruction of fleet, 172; extension unaffected by British navy, 188 – 189; results of naval victory, 191; trade with Russia, 197–198; military relationship to British Isles, 204; cause of expansion, 205–206; character of war preparation, 207–208; scene of war with Britain, 210, 213; causes of inequality between British Empire and, 223; occupation of neutral frontiers of, 226–227.
Gibraltar, 142.

HAWAII, 92.
Herat, 199–200.
Hindu-Kusch, 198.

INDEX

Hoangti, 17.
Holland, 11-12.
Hongkong, 67, 93, 117.

IMPERIAL SOLIDARITY, 82-84.
India, frontiers, 3; conquest of ancient empires, 46; close association with continuance of British Empire, 48; principles on which tenure of depend, 49-51; relationship of population to landed area, 54-55; natural expansion of, 56-62; strategic position of, 63-65; importance to British Empire, 66-69, 73; vulnerability of frontiers, 91; interests in common with China, 95, 97-99; Japanese alliance no protection against Russia, 96; Russian expansion toward, 108-109, 112, 113-115, 117-118, 121, 126-127, 157, 182, 189, 191, 194, 199, 215; relation to British sea power in East, 175; laws governing defense of, 198, 199, 201, 204; weaker than Russia, 238.
Indian Ocean, 72, 175.
International alliance, 86-87.
Italy, 123-124, 136, 140, 214.

JAPAN, military superiority of, 41; unaffected by wealth of United States, 42; territorial expansion convergent upon India, 59-60; strategic position of, 63, 75-76; growth unsuspected by Russia, 85; alliance with Great Britain, 87, 96; potentialities of in Pacific, 88-91; danger to America, 92; essentials of national power in, 93-94; relation to equilibrium of Pacific, 95; natural ally of Russia, 97-98; significance of Japanese victory to Russian expansion, 112, 116-117, 121-122; interests not antagonistic to Germany's, 124-125; results to, from British defeat, 126; aggression against British Empire compared to Germany's, 127; sovereignty over Pacific necessity to, 156-157; unimportance at beginning of nineteenth century, 153; absorption of Korea, 141, 160; in Russian war, 168, 170, 172, 191; national mind militant, 192-193; contest with Britain must be naval, 204; violation of Korea's neutrality, 228-229; stronger than Australia, 238.
Jena, battle of, 171.
John III., King of Portugal, 11.

KABUL, 65, 199.
Kamchatka, 109.
Kars, 109.
Keang-tung, 110.
Kharakof, 200.
Khiva, 109,
Kiel Canal, 215.
Korea, 46, 76, 93, 141, 160, 228, 229.

LAW OF NATIONAL ENVIRONMENT, 45.
Leipsic, battle of, 171.
Lisbon, 227.
Louis XIV., 85.

MACEDONIAN EMPIRE, 41.
Madeira, 227.
Malay Peninsula, 57, 64.
Malta, 67.
Manchu Empire, 41.
Manchuria, 76, 111.
Mauritius, 64, 67.
Mediterranean, the, 67, 126, 143, 146, 175, 176, 214.
Melbourne, 78-79.
Mesopotamia, 115.
Mexico, 46.
Military preparedness, 216-224.

Mohammed, 42.
Mongol Empire, 41.
Monroe Doctrine, 40, 47, 146.
Moscow, 112, 116.
Moslem Empire, 41.
Mukden, 103, 112.

Napoleon, 42, 85, 106, 132, 135, 140, 153.
Narva, 112, 120.
Netherlands, the, 11; dangerous position of, 46, 137; strategic importance to Germany, 141–146, 160–161; limits British and German base of war, 213; importance to British Empire, 215.
New South Wales, 79.
New Zealand, 64, 67, 69, 72–74, 78.
North Sea, 145, 215.

Orange Free State, 73.

Pacific Ocean, 63, 67–69, 72–73, 85, 88–89, 108–109, 112–113, 116–118, 120, 126–127, 156–157, 175, 194–195.
Palestine, 45.
Pamir, 95.
Paris, 112, 135.
Peace, natural laws determining, 22–24.
Persia, dangerous position of, 46; as affected by Indian expansion, 57, 65; wars with Russia, 109; Russia's expansion toward, 112, 114–116, 118, 120–122, 127, 157, 201, 204; possible area of Russian-British war, 191, 194–195, 199, 226.
Persian Gulf, 114.
Perth, Australia, 78–79.
Peru, 46.
Philippines, 92–93.
Poland, 45, 107–108.
Poltava, 112.
Port Arthur, 93.
Port Said, 65, 115.

Portugal, 11–12, 174.
Prussia, 141, 160.
Punic Wars, 90.

Queensland, 80.

Red Sea, 120.
Rhine, 215.
Roman Empire, 41.
Russia, 15; emigration to United States, 35; wealth compared to India's, 48; territorial expansion in relation to India, 59–60, 65; continental state, 75–76, 167; onward movement of, 85, 105–122, 201; conditions resulting from defeat by Japanese, 88–89; frontiers contiguous with China's, 95; China's expansion not antagonistic to, 96; natural ally of Japan, 97–98; not antagonistic to Germany, 124–125; result to from British defeat, 126; aggression against British Empire, 127–128; law of expansion, 130–132; position after Waterloo, 153; development in Asia, 157; advance on India, 182, 200; unaffected by British navy, 189, 191, 194–195, 204; economic relations with British Empire, 196–198; advance in Turkestan sphere, 199; in Mediterranean, 214; in relation to Denmark, 215; occupation of neutral frontiers, 226; violation of neutrality by, 228; relation to India, 238.

St. Petersburg, 116.
Samarkand, 199.
Saratof, 200.
Saxon, and Empire, 1–5; and war, 6–24; and America, 25–43; and India, 44–65; and Pacific, 66–81; and Eastern Asia, 82–99; and the Russian,

INDEX

100–118, 186–201; and Europe, 119–128; and the Germans, 129–146, 202–215; recession of, 149–163; sea power of, 173–185; necessity of offensive policy to, 220–227; military consolidation necessary to, 230–241.
Scheldt, 215.
Schleswig-Holstein, 141.
Sea power, 156.
Sedan, battle of, 171.
Seven Years' War, 12.
Seychelles, 64, 67.
Siberia, 116.
Sinclair, Sir J. G. T., preface.
Singapore, 64, 93, 117.
Slav, 41.
South Africa, 35.
South America, 145–146.
Spain, 11–12, 41, 136, 174, 214.
Straits Settlements, 64, 67.
Suez, 67.
Sviatosloff, 107.
Sweden, 107–108, 112, 121.
Sydney, 78–80.

Teheran, 65, 115.
Texas, 136.
Tibet, 46.
Tilsit, treaty of, 113, 140.
Transvaal, 73.
Tsar Alexander, 114.
Tsar Alexei-Michaelovitch, 107.
Tsar Boris Godunoff, 108.
Tsar John III., 107.
Tsar John IV., 107.
Tsar Peter the Great, 114, 132.
Tsar Theodore-Ivanovitch, 108.

Tsu Shima, straits of, 77.
Turkestan, 199.
Turkey, 75, 107–109, 113, 214.

United States, emigration to Canada, 32–33; relation to British Empire, 34–36; quality of population, 40; wealth of, 42; military relationship to Europe and Asia, 68; blind to changing military conditions, 69; possesses certain characteristics of an insular power, 75; indifference to Japanese development, 92; expansion against Canada unsuccessful, 130, 238; revenue of, 136; relation to German expansion, 137; unimportance at opening of nineteenth century, 153; land transportation of, 194; gradual abandonment of confederated government, 241.
Ussure, 109.

Valor of Ignorance, The, preface, 14, 91–92, 127, 144, 152.
Venice, 11.
Vicksburg, battle of, 171.
Victoria, Australia, 79.

Wagram, battle of, 171.
Waterloo, battle of, 153, 154.
Wei-Hai-Wei, 93.
Wu Tai Mountains, 16.

Zealand, 227.

THE END